The General Theory of the Translation Company

The General Theory of the Translation Company

The first ever book about the language services industry that won't bore you to tears.

Renato Beninatto & Tucker Johnson

Copyright © 2017 by Renato Beninatto and Tucker Johnson

All rights reserved. No part of this book may be reproduced in any form or by any electronic or mechanical means, including information storage and retrieval systems, without permission in writing from the publisher, except by a reviewer who may quote brief passages in a review.

www.nimdzi.com

Second Edition: December 2017

ISBN 978-0-9992894-1-9

Photography on back cover by Martina Wärenfeldt and Hugo Solomon.

From Renato
To Elcy, my mother, for making me yearn for the World.
To Sophia and Luca, my children, for being my motivation.

From Tucker
To Awo, my wife, who put up with many late nights at the laptop while writing this book.
To my children, Connor and Garry, who are my driving inspiration to follow my dreams.

Contents

INTRODUCTION, 1

Presenting the General Theory of the Translation Company, 8
Introduction to Market Influencers, 12
Introduction to Support Activities, 13
Introduction to Core Functions, 15

PART I - LAYING THE FOUNDATION, 17

A High-Level Look, 19
Defining the Language Services Industry, 19
Structure of the Industry, 20
Defining Your Niche, 23
Operating with Little Information, 34

The Five Market Influencers, 41
Threat of New Entrants, 43
Threat of Substitutes, 61

Bargaining Power of Customers, 78
Bargaining Power of Suppliers, 87
Industry Rivalry, 95
Defining Your Niche, 106

PART II - INTO ACTION, 109

The Seven Support Activities, 111
Management, 114
Culture, 116
Structure, 119
Finance, 123
Facilities, 125
Human Resources, 127
Technology, 129
Language Quality Assurance, 132

The Three Core Functions, 134
The Vendor Management Core Function, 138
The Project Management Core Function, 155
The Sales Core Function, 171

Getting to Work! 193

ACKNOWLEDGEMENTS, 195

GLOSSARY, 199

The General Theory of the Translation Company

Introduction

Welcome to the language services industry!

If you are already an industry veteran, then welcome to your opportunity to get a new perspective on the industry! It is a good place to be. We have fun here and we hope you will as well. And why wouldn't you? This is by far the most fascinating industry in the world. We, the writers, Renato and Tucker, have dedicated decades of our lives to localization. It is not just a job, not just a career, but also a passion and a way of life. There is no other job on the planet that could lure us away (it turns out "space cowboy" is not a thing yet).

We have chosen to write this book for two reasons: to teach and to have fun (not necessarily in that order).

Why teach? What do we want to teach? And whom do we want to teach? Let's explain.

Typically, translation is a lot like toilet paper. Nobody ever thinks about it until it is not there and nobody really knows how much it costs. This has allowed the language services industry to largely fly under the radar for decades, serving humbly in the background and letting our clients take the credit for the work we do.

But now, the industry is changing. Those of you who have been around a while know that this is nothing new. The industry is always changing. But there is a difference now: it is starting to mature and people from outside the industry are noticing. And they are very interested in what they see.

More and more companies are turning their eyes towards global domination and fresh faces are entering the industry every day. Back in the Stone Age when we started working in localization, nobody ever chose to enter this career. Ask anybody who has been around the industry before George Bush was in office why and how they got started in localization. Most will simply shrug, smile, and say, "Funny story, actually..." At which point, you should run. Run fast. Despite what they say, it will not be a funny story. It will be long and boring.

The point is that in days past, this was not a mature industry that people aspired to join. People just used to land up in this industry. Today, they climb into it. There were no school children dreaming of becoming localization project managers when they grew up. Today, multiple college courses and degrees prepare young aspiring language services professionals for a career in localization.

No single person or company founded the language services industry. Over the millennia, the industry evolved into what it is today and that evolution has happened almost completely organically. Until now.

Now, we are witnessing the adolescence phase of the industry. Outsiders are starting to recognize some of the big names in translation and it is not only when there is a major lawsuit in the news!

As the language services industry comes into its own, it has become apparent that there are some gaps that need to be filled. Particularly for young entrepreneurs who are starting out in the industry or industry outsiders who are perhaps interested in learning more about what goes on behind the scenes at a language services provider (LSP). For such interested parties, there is no single source of information available. Basic information that is so abundant in other industries seems to be missing when it comes to the language services industry.

In pursuit of our goal to teach, we are hoping to bring to the language services industry the same level of information and visibility that we take for granted in other industries. This is an overly ambitious goal for one book, but we predict that in the days to come, we will see more and more readily available information about language services. Eventually, this book will be a drop in the bucket. But we hope that by publishing early, we are able to influence, even if only in a very small way, the way information is taught, shared, and learned in the industry.

Our second goal for writing this book is to have fun. In case we haven't mentioned it already, we really love the language services industry. This book can be seen as our best attempt to convey our passion and enthusiasm for all things localization. If we were poetically inclined, we would call it our love letter to the language services industry. We both have very short attention spans, but somehow, we have been able to stick around in this industry for some time now, which can only mean that we are still having fun. It never gets boring!

So we are not ashamed to say that publishing this book is largely a selfish endeavor. We could claim that we feel a solemn responsibility to share our experience with the world, but, really, we also want to have fun and this seems like a neat little challenge for us! It is important to be upfront about this motive because it will undoubtedly affect the way you read this book.

Because, even though this book contains a lot of useful information, it is not a textbook. It has not been written like a textbook, nor should you read it as one. Textbooks are boring and unexciting. There is no passion in textbooks. This book? It's an extension of ourselves, Renato Beninatto and Tucker Johnson. There is no way we would write this without the passion we have for language services. Also, we like simplicity and short sentences. Really short sentences. Easy to write. Easy to read. Very easy. See? That's another reason this book will not fit in the textbook category.

This book is our attempt to provide information about the language services industry to those who are thirsty to learn more and to deliver it in a way that will not bore you to tears. Out of necessity, some chapters may be a bit more "dry" than others. We encourage you to hang in there. There needs to be some meat on the bones, and we will attempt to deliver that meat in as palatable a format as possible.

We will not teach you how to manage a glossary or internationalize your code. There will be no discussion on how to run a third-party quality assurance review, manage a website localization project, or set up an onsite interpreting project. This book is not about the "how". It is about the "what" and, most importantly, the "why" of the language services industry. There are plenty of other, if much more boring, books that will happily regurgitate localization best practices for over 500 pages. So if you are interested in the "how", then you may need to look elsewhere. However, since you've presumably already paid your hard-earned cash for the book you are holding, we invite you to stick around to see what you can learn.

This book will help the small business owner understand how to better grow their business. This book will inspire the young (or old) entrepreneur who wants to get into the language services industry. This book will help any and every employee working for a language services provider better understand how he or she adds value to the localization process. This book will encourage curiosity. It will raise questions. It will not provide all the answers, but it will provide us all with a common language to be used to frame better questions. It will facilitate a discussion between industry veterans, young entrepreneurs, language services buyers, investors, and anybody else who is interested in learning more about how to survive and thrive in the most fascinating industry on earth.

Presenting the General Theory of the Translation Company

Surely, you've heard the name Keynes, right? John Maynard Keynes was the most influential economist of modern times, so you've probably at least been exposed to the name before. When you hear somebody talking about Keynesian economics at a party, you may not know enough to join into the conversation. But you've heard of it, which means you know just enough to smile, nod, and then excuse yourself to go find a more interesting conversation.

Don't worry, we aren't going to focus too much on this subject. All you need to know to get our point here is that Keynes published his big claim to fame in 1936 under the title The General Theory of Employment, Interest and Money (or "TGTEIM", as nobody except us calls it, ever). And people haven't stopped talking about him since. His theory defined the conversation in his field for the next century. It challenged the long-held classical economic theories of the time and sought to bring about a revolution in economic studies.

Not everybody agreed with it, but everybody was talking about it. It forced the conversation away from the status quo and opened people's eyes to a whole new way of approaching a long-established discipline.

It is with unapologetic lack of both humility and self-awareness that we therefore would like to do the same for the language services industry as Keynes did for the field of economics. We present to you the General Theory of the Translation Company. Please hold your applause. We have a lot of ground to cover here.

Our Theory is not entirely new. However, there are some new concepts that we present, some that we recycle, and some that are just plain borrowed from other sources. The General Theory of the Translation Company was born as a sudden spark of inspiration for Renato years ago during a dinner conversation with a colleague wanting to better understand the industry. Renato took out a napkin and scribbled down the key components of the Theory, which we identify in this book as Market Influencers, Support Activities, and Core Functions.

Later, Renato would further formalize the Theory while working at Common Sense Advisory by publishing his ideas for the whole industry to study. In the years since then, he continually worked on it. When Renato and Tucker teamed up to write this book, Tucker brought his own ideas and experience to the conversation and the Theory was refined further. But at the heart of it, the General Theory is basically the same as when it was first written down on that cocktail napkin years ago. Concepts have been sharpened and the structure has changed a little, but the basic tenets have not changed. They have not needed to change because they have withstood the test of time.

The value of the General Theory of the Translation Company isn't so much that it presents new information, but that it presents information in a new way that allows us to take a more critical look at the language services industry and our place in it. Perhaps this won't start a revolution, but it can pave the way for a more critical analysis of our industry, which is long overdue. We need to start a new discussion in the industry and the General Theory of the Translation Company provides the framework for such a discussion.

In the sections to follow, we examine the language services industry and the three components of the General Theory of the Translation Company, which are the Market Influencers, LSP Support Activities, and Core Functions. As we conclude our discussion on Market Influencers, we take the next step to narrow the conversation and look at LSPs and how they operate within this ecosystem. In the subsequent section, we narrow our focus to Core Functions of the LSP and how these work to add value to the language services value chain. First, though, let's start out with a high-level overview of the General Theory of the Translation Company to provide some much-needed context.

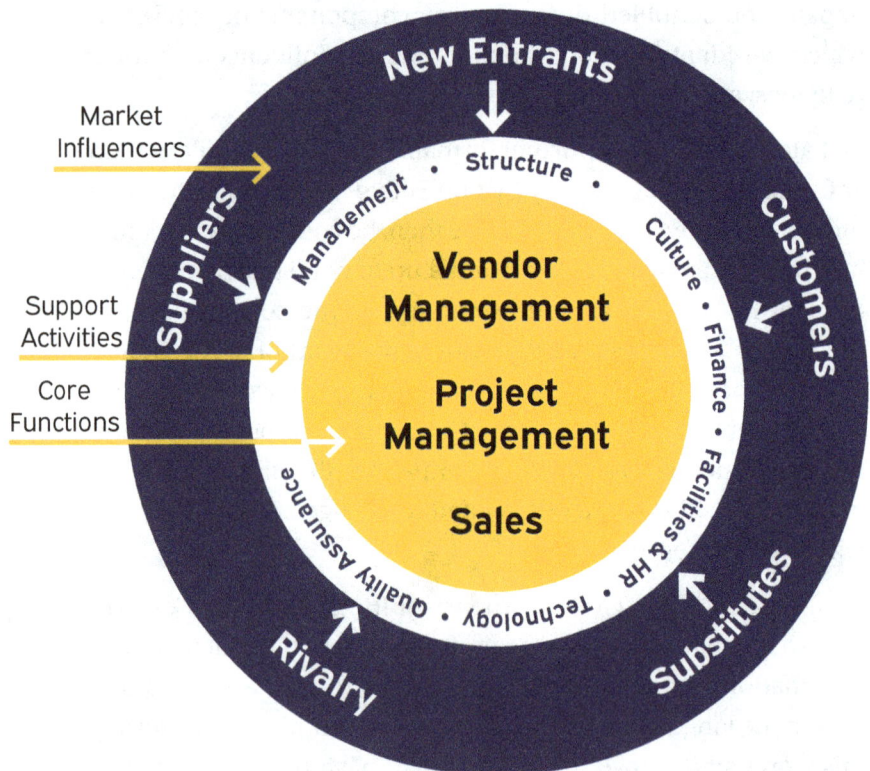

Figure 1: A visual depiction of the General Theory of the Translation Company.

As you can see from Figure 1, the General Theory of the Translation Company is broken down into three separate components, starting at the outside of the model with Market Influencers, then moving inward to Support Activities and then Core Functions at the center.

The flow from the outside towards the center is intentional. Successful LSPs always take this approach of starting with market analysis, and then using the information to set up Support Activities and structure that enable their Core Functions to add the maximum amount of value. Any other order of doing things is putting the cart before the horse.

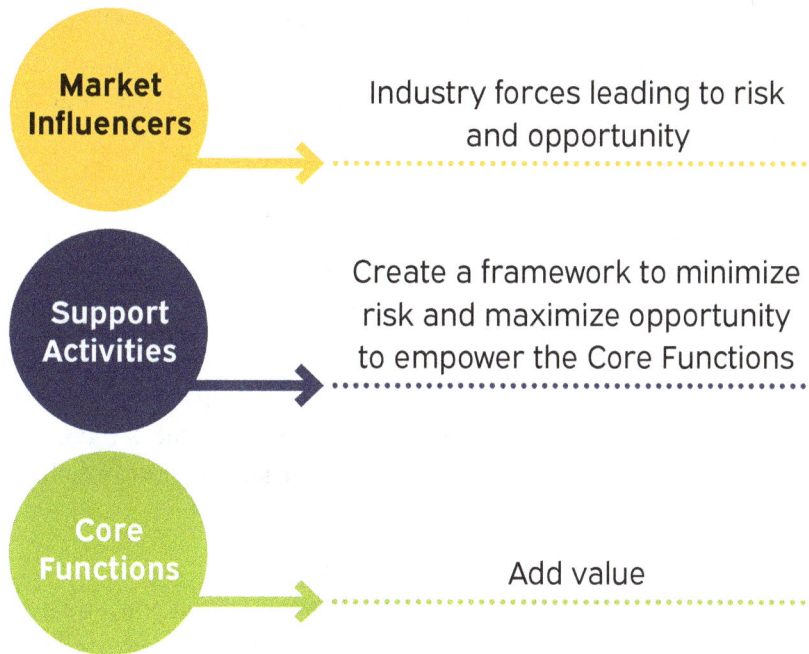

Figure 2: The three components of the General Theory of the Translation Company and their roles.

Evaluation of the Market Influencers reveals the forces that are leading to risk and opportunity. This is then used to define and set up Support Activities to minimize risk and maximize opportunity.

Finally, the Core Functions are those activities that are carried out by the LSP to add value.

Since the Core Functions are where value is created, you may be tempted to skip the other sections in the book. However, we beg you to be patient. There is a reason we do not start with the Core Functions.

If you are a project manager who is thinking of starting your own company, you can't just go out and project manage your way to fame and fortune. You need to slow down and make sure you are thinking strategically to set up an infrastructure that is going to allow you to scale your business. And it all starts with evaluating the Market Influencers. Likewise, if you do not set up and maintain the necessary Support Activities to support your Core Functions, you will find yourself struggling to deliver any value and will soon be out of business.

Or you could be the owner or CEO of an already established LSP and are experiencing aggressive growth. Perhaps you are worried that your company may not be able to sustain the growth and so want to take the time to ensure that you are setting your teams up for success. By using the principles in the General Theory of the Translation Company, you evaluate the competitive landscape in which you are operating, and put in place the strategy and structure that your LSP needs to continue sustainable growth.

Introduction to Market Influencers

Market Influencers are the five forces that shape and mold the language services industry: new entrants, substitutes, the bargaining power of customers and that of suppliers, and industry rivalry. By definition, the Market Influencers are largely outside of the control of any individual LSP. It is not our job to control or tame these market forces, but it is our job to observe and analyze them. We spend quite a bit of time on this topic in the book because it is critical to the success of the LSP. It is the first component of our Theory and it sets the stage for our discussions on Support Activities and Core Competencies.

Studying and evaluating the Market Influencers is like reading the tide chart and checking the weather report before you set sail. You may be one of the best sailors in the world, with the sturdiest boat ever built, but it is still important to make sure you know which way the current is flowing.

> **The 5 Market Influencers**
> 1. New entrants
> 2. Substitutes
> 3. Bargaining power of customers
> 4. Bargaining power of suppliers
> 5. Competitive rivalry

The Market Influencer evaluation is largely an intellectual step. There are no decisions or actions required, just evaluation. Just like with any analysis, it is only useful to the extent that it allows you to make decisions and act. It gives you the information you need to start defining how your LSP is going to be structured, which will manifest in the setup and maintenance of the senior management and other Support Activities.

Introduction to Support Activities

In the context of the General Theory, we define Support Activities as activities or functions that are carried out to enable your Core Functions to add value. We discuss the Support Activities after we finish our discussion of the Market Influencers because how you structure and carry out Support Activities should be a direct result of your evaluation of the Market Influencers. Performing your own evaluation of the market and identifying your niche allows you to make strategic decisions about where and how much to invest

> **The Seven LSP Support Activities**
> 1. Management
> 2. Structure
> 3. Culture
> 4. Finance
> 5. Facilities & HR
> 6. Technology
> 7. Quality Assurance

into Support Activities that will, in turn, strengthen your Core Functions.

Support Activities, by themselves, do not contribute to the language services value chain, except to the extent that they enable the Core Functions to add value. Basically, these are the activities, processes, structures, facilities, and services that foster an environment where the Core Functions can add value.

So, it may be tempting to downplay the importance of the Support Activities for an LSP, since we have made it abundantly clear that they do not directly add value. Keep in mind, though, that the value-adding Core Functions cannot be carried out in a vacuum. They require a proper environment to exist. Support Activities set up and maintain the environment to allow the Core Functions to be carried out.

As an example, consider the project manager who does not have a working computer because there is no IT department, or the vendor manager who cannot recruit anybody because the vendors are not getting paid. How long can a salesperson properly do their job, if there is no finance department to pay for client visits? To say that Support Activities do not add value is not to say that they are not important. Without these Support Activities, nothing happens.

Support Activities are not tied to any specific role. It is entirely possible for one person to be performing multiple Support Activities. For example, in a small LSP, the owner may take care of the accounting, human resources management, and other functions without any other help. In larger companies, there may be multiple departments for these same functions. Size is just one way in which LSPs differ. Of course, different companies may have different strategies or operate in unique niches.

We talk in detail about the seven necessary Support Activities needed in an LSP. This list is not meant to be comprehensive, as each LSP is different, but will showcase some of the more prominent Support Activities that are common to most LSPs.

Introduction to Core Functions

The three Core Functions are project management, vendor management, and sales. They are the meat and potatoes of the LSP. This is where value is added. If the Support Activities are what allow for the LSP's existence, then the Core Functions are what justify the LSP's existence.

> **The Three Core Functions**
> 1. **Vendor management**
> 2. **Project management**
> 3. **Sales**

And, project management is the most crucial function of the LSP. This isn't to say that other Core Functions (or Support Activities) are not important, but rather to emphasize that project management has the potential to most powerfully impact an LSP's ability to add value to the language services value chain.

Now let's just take a moment to call out the elephant in the room here. You're probably wondering why the General Theory classifies sales as a Core Function and not a Support Activity. How does sales add value to the customer? Isn't it all about making more money for the LSP? Or maybe you're thinking that quality assurance certainly adds value. You may even be thinking that quality is the only thing that adds value. Shouldn't it be reclassified as well, into the Core Functions? Don't worry, there are very good reasons to these and

any other questions you may have. A more in-depth explanation on the subject is found in Part 2 of this book, so you will have to be patient to learn more. For now, we will resist the urge to disclose any spoilers -- don't want to ruin the ending for you. Before we talk about adding value, we need to look at the market as a whole. First things first.

It is for this reason that this book is divided into two main sections. In Part 1, we present the language services value chain and provide critical background information to help you perform your own Market Influencer evaluation, define a niche, and build a solid foundation for a competitive and profitable LSP. In Part 2, we take a closer look at how LSPs set up their Support Activities and Core Functions to add value and remain profitable.

Remember that whether you are a translator, a project manager, or a CEO, you have a role to play in the language services value chain. The LSP's primary job is to add value. By understanding each (and all) of the three components of the General Theory of the Translation Company, you will better understand what role you play in accomplishing this goal. So sit up straight, pay attention, and let's get to work.

Part 1 : Laying the Foundation

A High-Level Look

Defining the Language Services Industry

So what exactly are we talking about when we discuss the language services industry? We need to take a moment to explain, because perhaps some of our readers are industry outsiders or maybe just getting into the industry. Even if you are an industry veteran, it's important for us to frame the discussion before getting much farther, just to make sure we are all on the same page.

To define the industry, let's first define the services included in this broad category. Technically, language services can include anything that has to deal with, well, language (we like to not over-complicate things here). We realize this is a broad definition, so for the purposes of this book we are going to refine this definition some more. The language services industry includes any and all business related to helping language services buyers (LSBs) to adapt or create content, products, or services in order to better compete in the global marketplace. This includes translation, internationalization, localization, interpreting (both in person and over the phone), global market research, multimedia adaptation such as voice over, dubbing and subtitling, marketing and branding localization, international consulting, software localization and related services, testing... the list could go on and on.

To fully understand the different services and the companies that provide them, we will break out this section into a short discussion of each of the major classes of service providers in the industry. These descriptions and illustrations are meant to be general only and may not accurately reflect your current position or offerings. Keep in mind that the localization services industry is incredibly complex and dynamic. It would take a thousand pages to even list a fraction of the different possible iterations of LSPs, and nobody wants to write (or read) a thousand pages of that.

So, what are the different types of providers we find in the industry?

- Massive multiple language services provider (MMLSP)
- Multiple language services provider (MLSP)
- Regional multiple language services provider (RMLSP)
- Single language services provider (SLSP)
- Freelancer or contract language professional (CLP)
- Language technology provider (LTP)

Structure of the Industry

There are as many different types of services in the language services industry as there are words in a dictionary. And there are as many different types of service providers and other key players as there are sentences written from those words. In this section, we discuss the various types of key players in the industry, starting with a look at the language services value chain, language services buyers (LSBs), and moving on to service providers including multiple language services providers (MMLSPs, MLSPs, and RMLSPs), single language services providers (SLSPs), and freelancers or contract language professionals (CLPs) which cover perhaps the widest array of players of them all.

The Language Services Value Chain

Each of these key players interact with each other in the

language services value chain, which we will discuss further in a later chapter, but deserves a brief introduction here. The language services industry is multi-layered, as can be seen from Figure 3. Each layer represents another intermediary service provider, as we will discuss in greater detail later in this chapter.

At first glance, it seems to just be an unnecessarily long chain of middlemen and outsourcing. One may ask that if a buyer needs translations, why wouldn't they just cut out the middleman and hire translators directly? By doing this, they could cut out the middlemen and reduce costs. But this would be a mistake. There is a very good reason why the industry has evolved this way, and the most basic way to describe it is by the concept of Core Functions and added value.

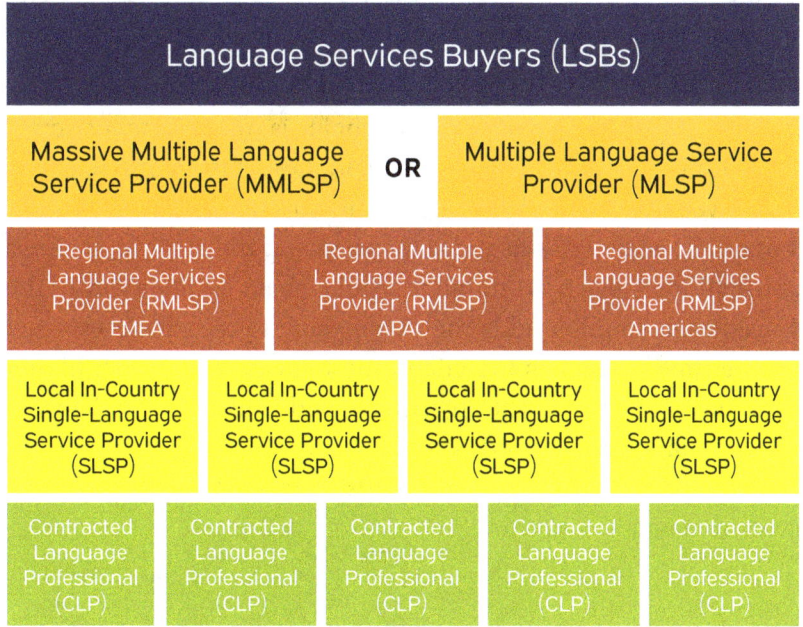

Figure 3: The language services value chain.

We need to clarify one thing up front. LSPs do not provide translation; they provide vendor management, project management, and sales. This may come as a shock to you. You may then ask why one would hire a language services company to provide translations if that is not even their core competency? The answer is because the industry is structured in such a way that each of those middlemen, or LSPs, add necessary value.

As we can see in Figure 5, each company in the chain adds value through its Core Functions. Along the way, each LSP also marks up the price of their services a bit so as to make a margin. The total value added at each step also reflects the value (in the eyes of the customer) provided by the LSP through their experience and expertise, which make the value perception even higher than the price being paid.

The language services value chain is the interconnected, branching chain of buyers and suppliers that work together to deliver all of these language services to the end client. At the bottom, freelancers add value by providing translation. As these translations move up through the value chain on their way to the buyer, each supplier adds their own value to the process so that by the time it reaches the client, the total value is much higher than the original translations. This added value is at the heart of the language services industry. It is why LSBs are happy to pay higher prices to work with MMLSPs instead of working directly with translators.

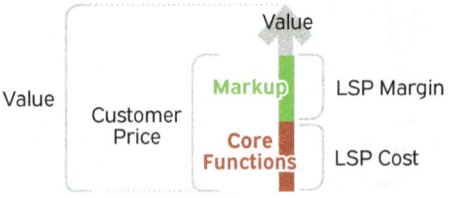

Figure 4: Each company in the value chain adds value through their core functions and marks up price to make a margin.

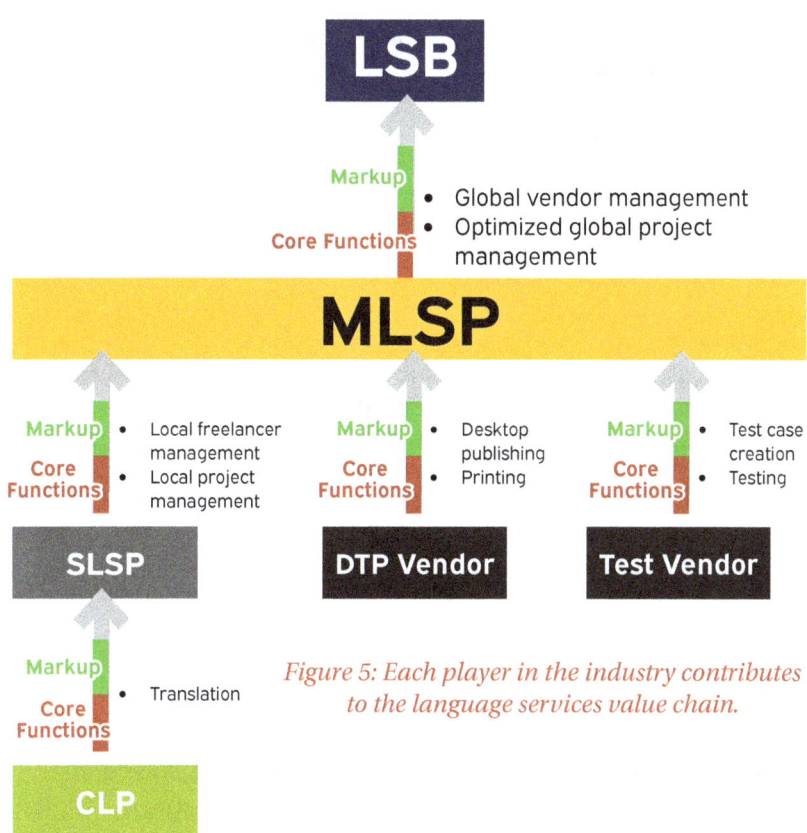

Figure 5: Each player in the industry contributes to the language services value chain.

If this seems complicated, don't worry. We will be discussing in more detail and providing specific examples as we move on through this book.

Defining Your Niche

You are holding this book, so you either already know or you are about to find out that the language services industry is a complex and dynamic environment. Specific demands originate with the LSBs and in time specialized services are developed by entrepreneurial-minded companies to meet these demands. This is one of the reasons the language services industry is so fragmented. It would be impossible for any one company to meet all of these demands on their own. The largest players in the industry, too, aren't able to do this and they rely heavily on their supply chain to supplement their own services.

> **DEFINITION OF NICHE**
> 1. **a.** a recess in a wall especially for a statue
>   **b.** something (such as a sheltered or private space) that resembles a recess in a wall
>
> 2. **c.** a place, employment, status, or activity for which a person or thing is best fitted · finally found her niche
>   **d.** a habitat supplying the factors necessary for the existence of an organism or species
>   **e.** the ecological role of an organism in a community especially in regard to food consumption
>   **f.** a specialized market

In this environment, there is a lot of opportunity for new or growing LSPs who are able to successfully carve out a niche for themselves. By specializing in a certain area that is in demand, they can lock themselves into a guaranteed revenue stream. See more on niches here.

If you are currently already working in the language services industry, then your company may have a very specific niche. If so, then the examples used in this book and the stories we tell may not relate to your experience 100%.

Now let's look at the key players in the industry and how they interact with each other in the language services value chain.

Language Services Buyers (LSBs) and Language Services Consumers (LSCs)

We will start our discussion at the top of the language services value chain by looking at the buyers and consumers of language services. We make a distinction between LSBs and LSCs: **the LSB**

is the ultimate purchaser of the languages services and the LSC, as the name suggests, is the ultimate consumer.

We don't need to spend much time talking about LSCs, because it is a relatively simple concept. In today's global economy, LSCs make up roughly ALL of the GDP of ALL of the global economies. In other words, we are all LSCs. You, us, the guy next door, the guy who sold you this book, your marriage counselor, everybody. Unless you are living off the grid deep in Appalachia, subsisting on creek water and squirrel meat, with a social life that consists of drawing faces on pine cones and hosting imaginary tea parties, I guarantee that you have consumed the end product of the language services industry.

Language Services Providers and Contract Language Professionals

Many have heard the term LSP before. It stands for language services provider (or localization service provider, depending on whom you ask). Generally speaking, this term will apply to any company in the language services value chain that adds value either through directly providing language services or by managing vendors of language services. The generic term LSP includes everything from a one-person translation company to a global multiple language services provider (MLSP) employing thousands. For the purposes of the discussions that follow in this book, though, it is necessary to draw a distinction between the different classes of LSPs that evolved in the industry.

In the past decades, we have seen translation companies grow from small regional agencies to large multinational enterprises, giving birth to the massive multiple language services provider (MMLSP). Much like the rise of the dinosaurs at the beginning of the Mesozoic Era, this phenomenon did not happen overnight (aren't you impressed with our dinosaur knowledge?).

Back in the early days when Renato was inscribing his

translations on stone tablets, LSBs would typically work directly with translators by hiring them internally or engaging them directly as freelancers or contracted language professionals (CLPs). Just like with the dinosaurs, though, a slow evolution occurred. Over time, some of these CLPs evolved into single language services providers (SLSPs), which evolved into regional multiple language services providers (RMLSPs) or MLSPs and eventually into the MMLSP – the Tyrannosaurus Rex of the Localization Kingdom.

Evolution doesn't occur autonomously. It is shaped by changes in the environment. The evolution from CLP to MMLSP was driven by the changing demands of the customers and other external market influencers. In our example, the MMLSP represents the end result of this process and is therefore the most evolved, but is no more important than any other players in the industry. It may seem like the king of the jungle, but it is only one player in a delicate ecosystem that is heavily dependent on other players.

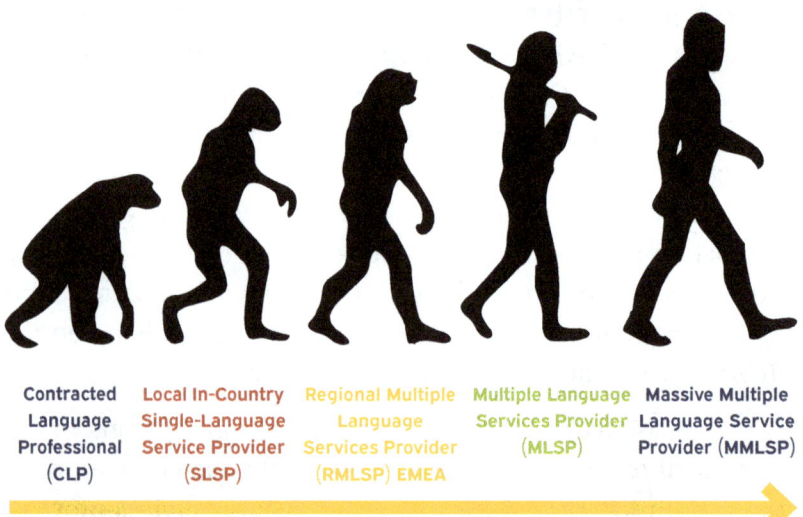

Figure 6: A probable evolution path for LSPs.

Figure 6 not only represents how LSPs have evolved as a species over the years, but also represents the typical path that a company may take as it grows in the industry. That is, if it is able to stay in business and not get bought by a third party.

So let's take a look at our typical value chain to examine the role of different classes of LSPs and see how they interact with each other. We will start at the bottom with CLPs and work our way up to MMLSPs. We frame the discussion this way so that we can see how one can grow out of the other, with the natural evolution from CLP to SLSP to RMLSP to MLSP to MMLSP.

Contract Language Professionals (CLPs)

The CLP is arguably the most important player in the entire industry. This category consists of any individual contributor in the value chain, but is primarily made up of translators, proofreaders, copywriters, marketing professionals, consultants, and engineers. It's basically anybody who has the skill and expertise to adapt content to global markets and is willing to sell their services. CLPs are the backbone of the language services industry. Without these unsung heroes, no work would get done.

There are many different types of CLPs in the industry today, but generally speaking there are some common traits among them. Many choose to work on freelance or short-term contract basis because it allows them the flexibility to set their own schedule, be their own boss, and have control over their work-life balance. On the other hand, some do choose to seek full- or part-time employment from a language services provider, and in some rare cases they work directly for the LSBs. Those who freelance set their own prices and reserve the right to choose what they work on and when they work on it. Many enjoy working as a CLP because it gives them the ability to work on multiple projects for multiple different clients, thus there is always something new and exciting to work on.

As we mentioned, it is increasingly rare to see CLPs working directly for the LSBs. LSBs used to contract directly with CLPs before the existence of LSPs, but over time LSBs' demands increased.

LSBs began to require more complex services such as project management and engineering, which was outside of the scope of most translation CLPs. So the industry evolved to meet these needs. Some CLPs chose to remain as individual contractors. Others chose to grow along with their clients into SLSPs.

The topics discussed throughout this book will be valuable to any CLP. If you are a CLP who is passionate about your work and enjoy the freedom that comes from freelance work, this book helps you better understand the larger marketplace in which you are operating. It gives you the knowledge and confidence you need to work for more interesting clients and make more money doing it. If you are interested in growing your business into an SLSP or MLSP model, this book can help you with that, too.

Single Language Services Providers (SLSPs)

Imagine you are a freelance translator working directly with a hot new computing company back in 1980. This promising new client of yours seems to be growing rapidly and soon has much more content than you can handle. You could A) try to translate faster yourself, or B) hire some junior translators to increase your capacity. If you choose option B, you then add a percentage to the rate you are charging the client and eventually you have a team of 20 translators working for you and are making a profit from the business without having translated a single word yourself. This is exactly how the first SLSPs came on the scene, and it was all in response to changing (read: increasing) client need.

SLSPs constitute the bulk of all translation agencies in the world (assuming of course, that we are including one-person operations, which are basically CLPs with a business license and better branding). This is largely because it is one of the most sustainable business models in the industry. It is a happy medium between the risks of being an independent CLP and the overhead of managing dozens of languages like an MLSP does. It is with this in mind that we decided that a lot of the data and ideas presented in this book will be directly relevant to SLSPs both large and small, new and old.

Regional Multiple Language Services Providers (RMLSPs)

Some SLSPs are not content with one language. There is more money to be made by offering multiple languages and LSBs were all too happy to let their suppliers provide even more languages for them. The incremental costs of adding additional languages are minimal in the grand scheme of things, especially if you are operating in a market with multiple language requirements and therefore have easy access to translators for other languages.

> **What RMLSPs Do**
> - Mostly operate in countries like India where multiple languages are spoken or deal with geographic clusters such as the Balkan or Baltic languages.
> - Specialize in lesser-known (lower demand) languages such as indigenous African languages.
> - Specialize in different dialects of the same language, such as different variants of Latin American Spanish.
> - "Virtual" RMLSPs specialize in different dialects of a language from different regions, such as Portuguese and Brazilian Portuguese, French and French Canadian.

RMLSPs came on the scene as soon as the technology and infrastructure was available to support such a business model. For example, 20 years ago, with the continually decreasing costs of travel and international communication via long distance telephone services, a Brazilian SLSP providing Portuguese translations could grow to provide Spanish translations with relative ease. In Europe, the fall of the USSR meant that some Eastern European SLSPs could expand into additional Eastern and Central European languages, thus multiplying their service offerings.

The RMLSP still exists today and is still a viable business model. These companies can add a lot of value, whether they are engaging with MLSPs or directly with LSBs, particularly in areas where there are multiple regional languages spoken or if they are specialized in rare languages. An MLSP would much rather contract with a single RMLSP in Southeast Asia, for example, than have to find separate vendors for each of the dozens of regional languages.

RMLSPs can operate in regions with obscure or hard-to-source languages. They carve out a niche for themselves and add value through their vendor management Core Function.

There are even some LSBs who prefer to contract directly with RMLSPs either because they are strategically focusing only on a single region for global expansion, or because they enjoy the reduced costs associated with cutting out the middleman that is the regular Multiple Language Services Provider. However, mostly RMLSPs will actually contract with the MLSP to perform their work, which gives them a steady and predictable flow of work without the overhead of having to actively acquire new LSB clients and maintain those relationships directly.

For RMLSPs, the information in this book is useful to understand a little more about the larger ecosystem in which they operate, as well as the specific value that they bring to the language services value chain. Specialized RMLSPs are a very important cog in the larger machinery of the language services industry.

Multiple Language Services Providers (MLSPs)

RMLSPs are technically MLSPs (with an additional letter in front of the acronym). For the purposes of this book, though, we draw a distinction between RMLSPs and MLSPs, as they operate in different niches in the industry and often have different customers. This is to say, they are both MLSPs but they rarely compete directly with each other. In fact, MLSPs are RMLSPs' biggest customers!

MLSPs oftentimes grow out of SLSPs or RMLSPs as they continue to offer more and more languages to their clients. However, it is equally common for MLSPs to start from scratch, completely skipping over the SLSP and RMLSP stage. As we discuss later, there is really no barrier to entry into this industry and anybody with a computer and a willing customer can become an MLSP from scratch.

The key distinguisher between MLSPs and other LSPs is that more and more LSBs are almost universally deciding to work exclusively with MLSPs, rather than either with smaller LSPs or directly with translators. This is part of the larger trend in the industry over the years that has moved translation from a local to a global industry.

Decades ago, if you needed translations, you would pick up the phone book to find a company. Almost without exception, these companies were small and specialized in one language. The yellow pages were the LSP's best marketing tool. Hundreds of companies like "AAA - Spanish Translation Agency" or "0-Errors French Translation" dominated the advertisements, each trying to stake a claim on that coveted first slot in the alphabetically listed directory.

All this changed with advancements in technology and lowering of barriers to global business. International phone lines, fax machines, then the world wide web and email - all these led to the natural and inevitable emergence of companies that could offer not only multiple languages from their region, but from countries all over the world. For an Argentinian LSP, it was suddenly just as easy to hire a Chinese translator as to hire a Spanish translator. This brought more value to the end-client because it meant that they did not need to manage as many vendors and could instead engage with a single vendor who could handle all of their localization needs. Thus the MLSP was born.

One characteristic of a typical MLSP is that they work with dozens of languages that are not confined to any geographical area. In fact, most MLSPs will not even have a set list of languages that they work with because they understand that by maintaining a structured and flexible vendor management program, they can effectively source any language required by their clients. Their typical answer to a client asking about which languages they offer is simply, "Depends. Which languages do you need?"

Another characteristic of an MLSP is that they work almost exclusively with LSBs. They rarely sell their services to other LSPs or any other players within the industry.

Even though MLSPs are at the top of the language services value chain, it doesn't necessarily mean they are always the biggest players in the industry. There is absolutely such a thing as a one-person MLSP. This is why we draw a distinction between an MLSP and an MMLSP (that is, Massive Multiple Language Services Provider).

MMLSPs are simply very large MLSPs. You would probably appreciate a more exact definition here, but we aren't going to give it to you. The absolute truth of the matter is that any distinction we draw would, at the end of the day, be entirely arbitrary. We could say MMLSPs are over X dollars in revenue or employ Y number of employees, but such a definition doesn't add value to our conversation here. Why? Because, in the language services industry size does not matter. Size is just a state of mind and when LSPs start to define themselves by their current size, they are unconsciously limiting their potential. So, our distinction between MLSPs and MMLSPs is only meant as a useful descriptor that we can use to frame the discussions in the rest of the book.

Regardless of size, MLSPs play a very important role in the language services value chain. They are the gatekeepers to the entire language services industry. Nine times out of 10, when an LSB approaches the industry for language services, they approach an MLSP.

Throughout this book, we use many examples to illustrate different concepts and a disproportionate amount of these examples focus on the MLSP. This is chiefly because the MLSP is the player in the industry that has both a relationship with the LSB (end-customer) as well as all other players from RMLSPs, to SLSPs and CLPs. Therefore, it is very useful to use MLSPs as examples when illustrating points that take the entire language services value chain into account.

Language Technology Providers (LTPs)

Language technology providers (LTPs) provide technical support that allows other types of service providers to do their jobs more efficiently. These LTPs are largely outside of the discussions in this book, but are an important part of the ecosystem and therefore deserve a mention here.

Language technology is constantly evolving and improving, and LTPs play an important role in this process. Undoubtedly, changing technology is one of the most important Market Influencers in the industry. However, in the book, we are going to refrain from diving too deep into the different types of language technology that are driving this change because our attempt here is to write a book that is general enough to be useful to everyone. If we were to include a current analysis of today's technology and its impact on the industry, this book would certainly be out-of-date within a matter of months. That is how quickly this specialized field is evolving.

We discuss the LTP's role in greater detail in subsequent chapters where we look at the effects technology and innovation have on Market Influencers, the role that technology plays in an LSPs' Support Activities, and how technology can be used to augment the value added through Core Services. If you currently work for an LTP or dream of bringing together your passions for technology and language one day, then this book may not tell you how to go about doing that. But it does provide invaluable insight into the industry in general and an idea of the buying behaviors of your potential clients, which could range anywhere from CLPs to LSBs.

Operating with Little Information

The language services industry is huge and encompasses many different types of LSPs, so it is impossible to get too deep into specifics while still having a discussion that is relevant to everybody. Another reason why we can't get too specific is because there just isn't enough information out there.

When we start discussing what we don't know about the industry, a pessimistic person (like Tucker) may point to this lack of information and see risk, but those with a more optimistic disposition (like Renato) will see nothing but opportunity. Regardless of how you see it though, it is undeniably important to at least recognize the inadequacy of available information about the industry because this allows you to proceed with a certain degree of caution. Regardless of whether you are a freshly graduated CLP looking for your first clients, or the CEO of a MMLSP and just closed a multi-year contract with God Himself, a certain degree of humility and caution should be taken as you navigate the market and work to carve out your own niche in the industry.

Before getting further into the General Theory of the Translation Company with the Market Influencers evaluation, let's take a moment to look at some of the factors that are limiting the quality and quantity of information available.

Lack of Outsider Analysis

Let's face it. Very few people actually know anything about the language services industry except for those of us in it. Business analysts are no different. They either simply give up because they have no idea how to measure it or try to force it into the same standards as other industries, which sometimes just don't apply to the languages services industry.

This means that the languages services industry isn't covered well enough by analysts and reporters. So, many of the normal channels that people would use to get information about an unfamiliar industry just aren't available. At the time of writing this, just a handful of publications and advisory agencies are attempting to meet this demand, but their efforts could not possibly suffice to provide the level of information that one has come to expect from, for example, the tech industry or the automotive industry.

There is a Catch-22 at play here. Nobody reports on the industry because it is not well understood and it is not well understood because nobody has taken the time to report on it. What this means is that the only people who are reporting on it are those from the industry, since they are the only ones who understand it properly. This can be problematic for two reasons.

- **Playing nice to avoid controversy.** Industry insiders are often reluctant to be critical of other players in the industry, for fear of rocking the boat too much. This means that critical thinking and skepticism are often thrown out the window in favor of recycled "headlines" and flattering commentary. Recycled headlines are popular because they don't have to be risky or controversial. Flattering commentary is favored because it is too risky to make any enemies. Ultimately, though, there is a deficit of any meaningful or actionable new information or insight into the language services industry.

- **Existing in the echo chamber.** We industry insiders have, over time, created a positive feedback loop – an echo chamber of sorts. This loop has led us to believe everything we hear. In the absence of contrary opinions, we have lost the ability to think critically about our industry.

You would be hard pressed to get too many industry insiders to admit it in mixed company, but this lack of outside analysis is a serious threat. The resulting groupthink compromises the credibility of the industry and serves to limit both the amount and quality of information available on the industry even further.

Lack of Publicly Available Information

When analyzing any industry or market, one of the most useful sources of information is the financial reports from publicly traded companies. In the language services industry, too, some of the most valuable data we have is from the annual reports submitted by MMLSPs and other publicly traded companies. However, these financial reports are few and far between because the reality is that there aren't a whole lot of publicly traded LSPs. The language services industry is so fragmented that small firms vastly outnumber large ones, and these small firms are less likely to be public or publish their financial data.

Financial reports may be interesting academically, but are not very useful to many LSPs unless they are directly competing in the same niche. For example, finding out that one of the largest MMLSPs is operating with a 25% operational margin may be interesting to learn, but this information is not going to be life-changing for most LSPs because they are operating in completely different niches and so it is not an apples-to-apples comparison. On top of this, it is necessary to keep in mind that LSPs operating in different countries are subject to different financial reporting requirements.

We Weren't Big or Interesting Enough

In the language services industry, the companies that actually are publicly traded haven't been very interesting to people outside the industry. This is not just because they do not provide an apples-to-apples comparison to other LSPs, but also because the vast majority of people in the world don't know or care about language services. This is changing. People are starting to become interested and many of them will buy this book to learn more. But historically, there has not been demand from the general public to report widely on the language services industry.

Top MMLSPs in the industry do business in the hundreds of millions, employing thousands of people around the world. Compare this to the top companies in other industries who do business in the billions and employ hundreds of thousands of people. Why would The New York Times even bother reporting on some no-name two-million-dollar LSP when Apple, Google, and Microsoft are valued in the billions and Amazon is sending people to Mars? The mainstream news covering an LSP would be like sending Anderson Cooper to report whether Punxsutawney Phil saw his shadow last February.

Dynamic Nature of the Industry

The language services industry is incredibly turbulent. It is constantly changing in size, structure, processes, and practices.

Just about the time somebody figures out how to manage and analyze data around any aspect of localization, everything changes and it's back to the drawing board. Even if we were to be able to report consistently year over year, it is hard to track any trends year over year because the yardsticks (or meter sticks, we suppose, for our international readers) we use to measure the industry are themselves being reevaluated and updated.

In the Introduction, we claimed that one of the goals of this book is to respond to a demand we have perceived for information. There is a great need for up-to-date information about the latest changes and trends in the industry. However, it is not the goal of this book to discuss the latest and greatest trends in the industry. Such discussions are better assigned to periodicals and online sources, because they require a greater deal of flexibility than the paperback printed format will allow. This book discusses the macro trends in the industry and, more importantly, provides a framework for discussions about the faster moving micro trends. We will not measure the moving target for you, but rather give you the tools and training to measure it yourself.

Number of Players in the Industry

There are a ton of players in the language services industry, which makes it somewhat hard to study and report on. If you want to follow the tech industry, you basically have to watch the big dogs (think Apple, Microsoft, Google, Tesla, Amazon, etc.) and the "up and comers". The latter are usually easy to identify because they are generally the latest vanity project of some C-level executive leaving one of the big dog companies.

Now let's compare that to language services. Most industry outsiders couldn't even name one of the top three largest LSPs in the industry. Hell, a lot of people who are in the industry can't even name the top three LSPs. This is because the largest LSPs really aren't that large. The industry is fragmented. Really fragmented. There are so many companies operating in the industry that reporting becomes problematic. Reporting on all of them is impossible because there are just too many. Reporting on one of them is inadequate because even the top players are not large enough to command any significant market influence by themselves.

Compare this to the laptop manufacturing industry, for example, where the top six laptop manufacturers make up a whopping 85% of the industry. If you are a business blogger, do you really think you are going to put the effort into learning about the thousands of LSPs in the industry just so you can write an article about something that (as we already established in the previous section) nobody even cares about? No wonder the language services industry doesn't get reported on! There are simply too many players to follow.

Planning with Low information

As you can see, we have a problem here. It seems that there are so many missing pieces to the puzzle that we couldn't possibly move forward with any meaningful discussion on the industry. We recognize this problem and you can believe us when we say that we are just as frustrated as you. So frustrated, in fact that we chose to write a book about it. We spend the remainder of our time here trying to build on what we know and how to identify opportunities in the areas where we have incomplete information.

What this means for you is that there is tremendous opportunity. When an industry is saturated with information, it becomes saturated with new players that, in turn, saturate it with ideas. This means there would be no opportunity for new entrants to break in with unique new services, or for existing companies to expand. Think about it… Where information is lacking, there is still opportunity to create something new and original.

"Easy for you to say," you may be thinking. But actually, this is what we are doing ourselves. Rather than complaining about the lack of quality information in the language services industry, we are seizing the opportunity and writing this book to meet an unmet demand. With the information in this book, you can confidently go out and seize your own opportunity!

The lack of information available on the language services industry is the reason why Market Influencer evaluation takes such a critical place in the General Theory of the Translation Company. The evaluation empowers us to analyze not only the industry as a whole, as we have done so far in this section, but our specific niche in the industry and how specific Market Influencers work to influence an LSP's ability to add value and make a profit.

The Five Market Influencers

In 1979 the Harvard Business Review published a paper by Michael E Porter called "How Competitive Forces Shape Strategy". The driving idea behind the paper was to outline a framework that businesses could use to analyze the competition within their industry. Porter argued that companies should take a look at the forces at play in their industry and see how they can potentially affect the profitability of their own company as one of the many players within that industry. By not only analyzing your industry but also your company's relationship with the industry, Porter argued, you could gain more insight into how you can become more competitive.

Let us illustrate how this is relevant here. In previous sections, we have already talked about how each player in the language services industry needs to define a niche for themselves in the industry. By defining your own niche, you guarantee that you will always be in demand and therefore be able to make a decent margin.

THE MARKET INFLUENCERS ARE INSPIRED BY MICHAEL PORTER'S ARTICLE IN THE HARVARD BUSINESS REVIEW, "THE FIVE COMPETITIVE FORCES THAT SHAPE STRATEGY." THESE INFLUENCERS ARE:

1. THREAT OF NEW ENTRANTS
2. THREAT OF SUBSTITUTES
3. BARGAINING POWER OF CUSTOMERS
4. BARGAINING POWER OF SUPPLIERS
5. INDUSTRY RIVALRY

Think of your niche as your own private island in the great sea of the language services industry. If you are just starting out and haven't found your island yet, you need help navigating your course. Careful evaluation of the Market Influencers, based on Porter's Five Forces Model, gives you the tools to map the waters, identify your island, and avoid the shark-infested waters. If you've already found your island, this analysis will help you to better understand your position on the map and how you can leverage this to your advantage.

A truly comprehensive explanation of Porter's Five Forces is outside the scope of this book, but we would highly encourage you to learn more for yourself All of Porter's work is available online (welcome to the 21st Century). Don't be a cheapskate - pay for the online Harvard Business Review Subscription or purchase the article and you will be glad you did!

THE MARKET INFLUENCER EVALUATION IS MEANT TO EVALUATE **YOUR POSITION** IN THE INDUSTRY.

We have slightly rebranded Porter's Five Forces to develop the Market Influencers of the language services industry, but the principles remain the same. The remainder of this section summarizes how the five Market Influencers – New Entrants, Substitutes, Customer Bargaining Power, Supplier Bargaining Power, and Competitive Rivalry – work together to influence the ongoing evolution of the language services industry. Each of these Market Influencers is driven by a number of factors and we discuss each one of these and the role they play in increasing or decreasing the power of the Market Influencers.

In the General Theory of the Translation Company, the Market Influencers surround the LSP and push inwards. These represent the forces in the language services industry that exert pressure on (and provide opportunities to) the LSP. It is up to the LSP to analyze and better understand how to structure the Support Activities that enable the Core Functions to create value.

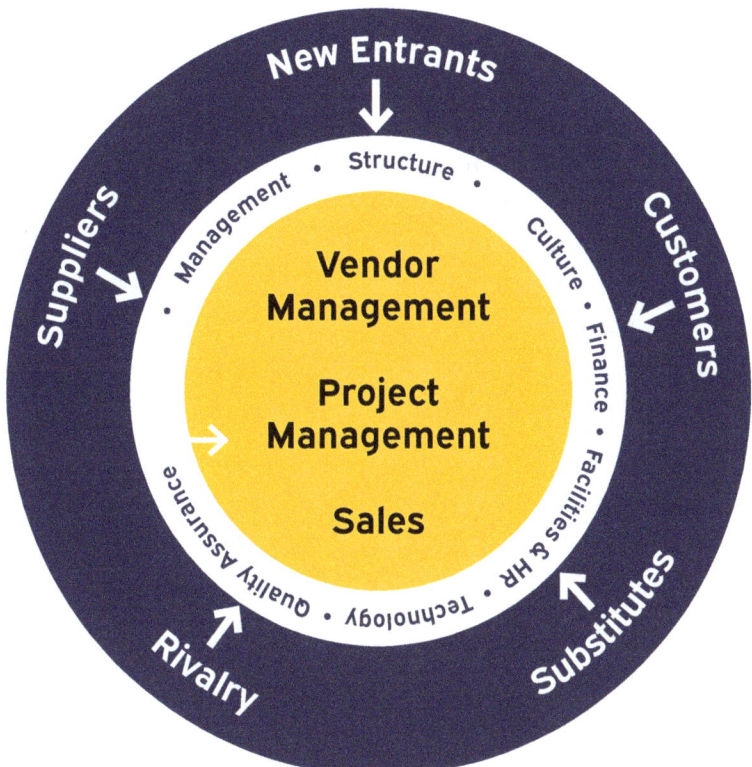

Figure 7: Market Influencers surround the LSP.

By the time we are through with this section, you will have the information and insight that you need to perform your very own Market Influencer evaluation. The Market Influencer evaluation is the first step in understanding not only the language services industry, but also how to define and execute a winning strategy for your company.

Threat of New Entrants

The first of the five Market Influencers affecting the language services industry is the threat of new entrants. If you have taken any business classes in the past, you may have also referred to this as the barrier to entry into an industry. When the barrier to entry is low, the threat of new entrants is high. Conversely, when there is a high barrier to entry, there will be little competition from new entrants.

Driving this threat of new entrants is a number of factors that should be taken into account when analyzing the industry. Depending on whom you ask, different experts have different lists, but in general, the following are the factors that affect how easy (or hard) it is for new companies to enter the market and directly compete for customers:

- Intellectual property (existing patents/trademarks/copyrights)
- Governmental influence and policy
- Brand equity (reputation)
- Customer loyalty
- Ease of switching providers
- Level of differentiation in products or services
- Economies of scale
- Profitability
- Capital investment costs

Intellectual Property (Existing Patents/Trademarks/Copyrights)

The language services industry is all about providing, well, language services. Services, as a rule, are something that are incredibly hard to patent or trademark. You cannot patent the act of translating any more than you could copyright a verb. This doesn't mean that translation companies haven't tried to get a competitive advantage by building and protecting their own intellectual property (IP). Usually this comes in the form of either patenting a technology or a certain workflow process. Most of the time, though, the technologies and the workflow processes are so interconnected that it is difficult to distinguish one from the other.

Technology, of course, can be a major factor for language technology providers (LTPs) whose core competency is developing and selling language software and tools. These tools usually take the form of computer-aided translation (CAT) tools, workflow and enterprise resource management (ERP) tools, or machine translation (MT) engines and the artificial intelligence (AI) that drives them. For the typical LTP, it is abundantly clear that technology can majorly influence the market relative to their niche. LTPs will want to guard their intellectual property fiercely, as this holds the key to their competitive advantage in the industry.

As for LSPs, most license software from one of the leading LTPs in the industry, rather than develop their own. However, many MLSPs and all of the MMLSPs in the industry have worked to develop their own tools so that they don't have to be reliant upon a third party for tools that are absolutely critical to their process. Additionally, LSPs seek to differentiate themselves from their competitors by having more efficient toolsets that can reduce internal costs, manage overwhelmingly complex and agile localization programs, and create value for end clients by easily integrating with the clients' systems.

Think of an MMLSP that is doing US $50 million in business with a large technology company in Silicon Valley. They were able to win the contract by convincing the client that their proprietary software adds more value than their competitors' solution does and that it will seamlessly integrate with the client's systems. The fact that the MMLSP alone holds the patent to this tool powerfully decreases the threat of a new entrant coming in and stealing the business. New translation companies just do not have the resources to quickly come up with equivalent, IP-protected tools.

A little further down the supply chain, we have CLPs working as freelance translators for the MMLSP. If they are translating using the MMLSP's toolset, then the threat of new entrants to them may be very high. If the MMLSP controls the environment in which the work is being performed, then it can at any time choose to replace any CLP with a cheaper newcomer. Basically, if you are working with tools or processes that are not your own, you are easier to be replaced with a new entrant.

The factor of intellectual property can be very powerful or virtually meaningless, depending on the position of the business you are in. For an LTP that develops CAT tools or an LSB that is investing in their own machine translation engines, IP is everything. However, a small LSP that uses standard processes and publicly available tools may not have any real IP to speak of. This is why it is impossible to provide a standard analysis for the industry as a whole and it is important to make sure to analyze it from the perspective of your business.

Governmental Influence

Typically, governmental policies depend on where a company is based. For the SLSP, the degree to which this factor will affect its position in the market is based entirely on where its company is registered, which even holds true to a certain extent for larger MLSPs. This is why it is so important to make sure you are thinking strategically about where to situate the headquarters of your company if you are planning on going global.

If you are working as a CLP for a small SLSP or RMLSP, you will want to look at your local country's laws and regulations, particularly those considering accounting practices, finance, and international contract law (see more on this in Part 2). For example, what are the reporting requirements for revenue in foreign currencies? Does your local government have any incentives that you can take advantage of? Are there any additional taxes that need to be paid for services rendered across national borders and if so, who is responsible for paying those?

When looking at the factor of governmental influence in the context of analyzing the threat of new entrants, you want to ask yourself the following question: does governmental influence make it easier or harder for new entrants to enter the market, compete within my niche, and drive down my profits?

To understand how governmental influence affects the threat of new entrants for global MLSPs and MMLSPs, you should essentially answer the same questions as above. Then answer them again. And again. And keep doing that until you've answered these questions for each of the multiple locations in which you are operating. This holds particularly true for contract and employment law, as labor laws vary wildly from country to country and it is not always possible to employ people in a foreign country without getting governmental approval or going through a local intermediary (thus reducing your margin). For a well-established MMLSP, the overhead and costs involved in legally employing a global workforce could effectively eliminate the risk of new entrants, depending on the type of work you perform and how you choose to contract with your employees.

If your business model is to employ full-time employees, then the barrier is high, but if you only need to contract with in-country SLSPs or CLPs, the barrier is once again very low. A further discussion on types of employment follows in the section on global human resources as a support service and the Core Function of vendor management.

Brand Equity

When we talk about brand equity, we are talking about perceived value. Two important sub-factors come into play here: brand awareness and brand reputation. The best-case scenario is that you have a good reputation and a high brand awareness, as you will be able to position yourself as a premium supplier, charge higher rates, and enjoy a healthy margin. However, if your reputation is poor, then you certainly have some work to do. Until you improve your reputation in the industry, you will be stuck begging for table scraps and your margins will be microscopic, if you are lucky enough to be making any profit at all.

It should be apparent how reputation and brand recognition can have real and lasting effects on any LSP competing within the industry. However, please allow us to go off on a slight tangent for a moment to discuss something that we feel is important, even if

Reputation

		Poor	**Good**
Brand Recognition	**High**	Delete all your social media profiles, legally change your name, and THEN go find another day job.	Enjoy it while it lasts and don't get cocky, Icarus...
	Low	Work a little harder to improve your reputation, or go find another day job...	Good for you. Now go hire a marketing director to grow your business!

it is technically outside the scope of this discussion. Let's forget about the company for a moment (even if you are the owner of the company) and take a look at personal brand equity.

While the same concepts apply, personal brand equity is something that is specific to you. While working for a company with a good reputation will naturally lend you some credibility, it is not necessary that your personal brand equity closely mirror that of your organization. It is possible for you, as an individual, to be working for a really bad company, but still maintain a good reputation and be well-known among your peers in the industry. Likewise, it is possible to have a high paying job for a powerful company and have a low personal brand equity.

We've seen very prominent examples of both of these scenarios throughout our careers and can attest to the prevalence of this phenomenon. If you have been around for long enough, we guarantee that at some point you have looked at a senior manager or a client and asked yourself, "How the hell did they get that position?" Sometimes the answer is simply that they have done a good job of managing their personal brand equity.

Sadly, though, we have also seen very talented and hardworking individuals get chased out of the industry because they failed to properly manage their personal brand equity. This is a small and unforgiving industry and once you have been labeled with a negative reputation (deservedly or not), it is very difficult to recover.

We apologize for going off on somewhat of a tangent here and thank you for your patience. We thought it important to at least point out how the concept of brand equity can be applied not only to the LSP, but at a personal level as well. The same holds true for many other concepts in this book.

Read more about brand equity in the section on sales Core Function.

Customer Loyalty

LSPs that are able to effectively manage their reputation can enjoy a certain degree of customer loyalty. Consider a customer that has been working with an MLSP for years and has developed a strong relationship of trust. The customer's loyalty is so strong that the customer would never consider switching vendors and awarding business to a new entrant. So the threat of new entrants is practically zero in this situation, right?

Not necessarily. What happens if the MLSP decides it needs to save some money and so it cuts bonuses for its employees? Probably not much. The employees may be mildly disgruntled but they keep on working and providing excellent service to the customer, who doesn't even notice any difference. But what happens when the MLSP does the same thing the next year, and the year after that?

Eventually, those employees are going to leave. Most of them will go work for competitors, surely, but some of them are going to start their own businesses. And when they do, the first phone call they are going to make will be to that old customer that has had a long-standing relationship with the MLSP.

Here's where the idea of personal customer loyalty comes into play.

It is important to note that people do not buy from companies, they buy from people. If you have a highlighter, then make sure you highlighted the previous sentence. When people leave a company, it is very possible that customers may follow them. More than one now-thriving LSP in the industry today has been started by a disgruntled employee leaving and taking customers along. Therefore, any in-depth analysis of customer loyalty needs to take into consideration not just the overall level of brand loyalty to a company, but also what and who is the driving force behind maintaining that loyalty.

It needs to be mentioned that the most official form of customer loyalty would presumably the signed contract. LSPs like to sign multi-year contracts because they think it provides a degree of stability, protecting against not only new entrants, but also against other competition as well. LSBs like to sign multi-year contracts because they can use this as leverage to demand lower rates from their suppliers. However, it is important to note that in the language services industry, contracts between top LSBs and LSPs are often completely meaningless for the LSP. The harsh reality is that LSBs break contracts as they see fit and LSPs almost never take any action. LSPs just roll over and let this happen every day.

The reason for this is because of the small-town nature of the industry, where reputation is everything. LSPs sometimes feel that if they were to complain about their clients breaching a contract, it would jeopardize a future opportunity to do business with them. This is another one of those quirky unwritten rules of the industry that baffles industry outsiders. Everybody knows it, but nobody acknowledges it. LSPs continue to compete for the coveted multi-year contract, as if it actually means anything, and clients continue to pretend as if it actually means something.

Ease of Switching Providers

Generally speaking, the larger and more complex the business relationship, the more difficult it is to switch providers. So, this is another factor that is heavily influenced by where your company falls on the value chain. Larger MLSPs tend to have more complex relationships with their customers, and so it is harder for their customers to switch. Freelancers, on the other hand, have very straightforward relationships with their customers, and so they can be replaced easily. Often you will hear this referred to as client "stickiness". The more difficult it is for a client to disengage from a current supplier, the stickier the relationship can be said to be. The stickier a piece of gum is, the harder it is to pick it out of your hair, right? Same concept applies.

Let's look at an example of an MMLSP performing millions of dollars worth of work for a very large LSB. Not only are they doing a lot of work, they are doing many different kinds of work. Of course they are providing translation services, but they are also providing local market consulting services, transcreation, multimedia localization and adaptation, and on-demand interpreting. They may be performing this work in-house, but more likely they are contracting with partner companies in their supply chain and simply managing the project. To tie everything up with a nice little bow, they have also fully integrated their internal CAT tools and workflow management systems with the client's systems.

STICKINESS IS A FUNCTION OF THE TOTAL VALUE YOU ARE BRINGING TO THE CUSTOMER AND THE PERCEIVED COST OF SWITCHING VENDORS.

To put it mildly, their

relationship is very complex and highly integrated, something that took years to accomplish. While this MMLSP may face some competition from existing industry rivals, they essentially face zero threat of a new entrant to the market coming onto the scene to steal their customer away. The amount of work it would require for a new entrant to build a comparable program is at best costly and at worst, just plain impossible without cooperation from the customer.

This necessary cooperation from the customer is precisely what we are referring to when we talk about the ease of switching suppliers. It is not the cost to the LSP that is relevant here, but rather the cost to the customer. If the customer wishes to switch to a new supplier, they would have to spend a lot of time and capital to facilitate the transition. The new supplier would need to be trained. New automations and integrations would have to be built between their workflow management systems. Most likely, there will be a period of time where they are paying two suppliers at once as there will be an overlapping period in which the old supplier must ramp down and the new supplier must ramp up. In this situation, switching vendors is certainly not easy.

With CLPs, though, the costs are much lower for their customers to switch. CLPs are rarely highly integrated with their customers (typically LSPs) and therefore can be easily replaced. Most MLSPs and SLSPs who work with CLPs design their systems so as to decrease the bargaining power of the CLPs and make them easily replaceable. This is another example like we discussed in the section on Intellectual Property where the lower we go on the language services value chain, the higher the risk of being displaced by new entrants.

Level of Differentiation

In a business context, when we talk about differentiation, we are discussing the act or process of creating a distinction between two or more products or services. Differentiation can happen internally within a company, when a company offers different versions of the same product in order to better appeal to different target markets. An example of this in the language services industry is if a translation company were to offer "premium", "basic", and "economy" quality levels of translation for different prices.

For the purposes of our discussion on the threat of new entrants, though, we refer mostly to the process of a company differentiating services or products from the services or products of other companies. That is, the process of offering different and presumably better services than other players in the industry.

Pop quiz time! What would you say is the best way to differentiate your language services from those of your competitors and any new entrants to the market? We're guessing that it didn't take you long to come up with an answer, which was probably that quality is the best way to differentiate. By providing the best quality, you can make sure that your customers do not leave you to do business with new entrants or other competitors, right?

Well, not really. In fact, it can be plain wrong. Quality is not a differentiator, it is a prerequisite. If you think you can survive by differentiating only on high quality, you will be in for a big disappointment.

Quality doesn't matter.

Yes, we realize the above is a pretty shocking statement, but hang in there. We will be elaborating upon this controversial statement in depth when we talk about the Quality Management Support Activity in Part 2. The reason we talk about this in the section on Support Activities and not in the section on Core Functions is precisely because providing quality does not directly add value. If you are finding this a hard statement to swallow right now, please just play along so that we can get through this. We promise it will all make sense later.

So if LSPs do not differentiate based on quality, what then

are their differentiators? Usually they differentiate on their level and types of service they provide to customers. If you are an LSB engaging with an MLSP, then you are paying a premium for the added layer of service (project management, engineering, vendor management, etc.) that is being provided. Differentiation is enabled by the LSP Support Activities, but is executed by the three Core Functions of vendor management, project management, and sales.

This is even important for CLPs to keep in mind. Even though you may be a CLP providing translations, you need to realize that your customers, whether they are LSBs or LSPs, aren't working with you because of the quality of your translations, they are working with you because of the service you provide that makes their life easier, such as delivering on time, not asking a lot of questions, or providing regular status updates. Customers can buy quality from anywhere. The reason they continue to work with you is because of the value you add for them.

Whether you are a freelance CLP or a CEO of an MMLSP, differentiating your service to protect against new entrants can be a struggle considering the extremely low barriers to entry into the industry.

WHEN RALPH REALIZED WHAT TYPE OF ANIMAL SHELTER HE WAS AT, HE DECIDED HE NEEDED TO QUICKLY DIFFERENTIATE HIMSELF FROM THE COMPETITION.

Differentiation needs to happen on value, not quality. This is a large part of what this book is about–finding out what creates value and identifying areas where you can differentiate your value offering to attract and retain customers.

Economies of Scale and Capital Investment Costs

We have grouped together two slightly different factors here because they are somewhat related. Economy of scale refers to the ability of a company to become more efficient as it grows in size. Capital investment costs refer to the costs a new entrant incurs in entering the market. These are related because as a company grows, the initial investment costs (overhead) will be spread across a larger amount of business, effectively lowering the cost-to-revenue ratio (which is just a fancy way of saying increasing margin).

Capital investment costs for this industry are incredibly low. There is practically zero barrier to entry for a newcomer to start a new business providing language services. We (Renato and Tucker) could decide tomorrow to go start our own interpreting company and there would be nothing standing in our way. For the price of a business license and a coffee maker, we could have our own company up and running almost immediately. On the first day of running our new business, we are thrilled at the small amount of capital investment needed to follow our dreams. On day two, though, the reality hits us that not only do we need to compete with existing competitors, but there is also a very real risk of new entrants popping up to compete for a slice of our pie.

It is important to point out that this applies to new startups. If you approaching your market analysis as an MMLSP, then most likely you are not concerned about such small startups entering the market because they are not competing in your niche. You are working on multi-million dollar projects that require the use of thousands of dollars of specialized tools, brick-and-mortar locations around the globe, and a global workforce of thousands of employees. There is just no feasible way that a new entrant can come into the market and compete in the same arena as you.

The capital investment costs are simply too high and you are leveraging economies of scale to make sure you are able to enjoy a higher margin and compete more aggressively on price. While all of this may be true, we urge you to not rest on your laurels. New startups in the language services industry can grow at astonishing rates, especially if they are financially backed by outside investment. We have seen new companies grow in a matter of a few years to be able to start stealing customers away from even the largest MMLSPs.

Profitability

Profitability is a good thing, right? Why else would you start your business in the language services industry if you were not expecting to make some money in return for your efforts? Sure, there are those attracted to the industry because they have an unquenchable passion for language, but typically those people aren't going to be getting rich in this industry. The whole point of performing the Market Influencer evaluation is to gain further insight into your position in the industry so you can better situate yourself and your business to maximize your profit margins. You may be wondering, then, why we would be labeling profitability as a factor that could potentially increase risk. It is indeed a little contradictory that high profitability can lead to lower profitability.

To understand how profitability can increase the risk of new entrants, we need to first take a look at basic economics of supply and demand curves. They date back to before man first traded fetid mammoth meat for a handful of shiny new arrowheads. Forgive us if this is giving you unwanted flashbacks to freshman year Econ-101 class. It is necessary to lay the groundwork here, though, and we promise to be brief.

The law of supply and demand states that price (and therefore profitability) is a function of the relationship between the overall supply of a given service or product and the overall demand for that same service or product in the marketplace. Basically, how many sellers + how many buyers + math = market selling price. Because the market determines the selling price, the forces of the market will always be working to drive all prices towards this point. If companies are selling at a price lower than the market price, then their desire for profits will drive up their prices to the point where they can maximize their margins. In order for a company to sell at a higher price than market price, they need to differentiate themselves somehow, but will face constant competition in the market that seeks to drive these prices back towards equilibrium.

These competing forces of supply and demand are most commonly depicted in a graph that lists the overall number of suppliers or quantity of a product on the X axis and the price on the Y axis. The intersection of the supply and demand curve represents the equilibrium price and number of suppliers for a given industry. The only ways for the market price to increase or decrease is if the supply and demand curves were to shift positions on the graph. This could happen by an increase or decrease in demand, which would be represented by the demand curve shifting, or an increase or decrease in the total supply, which would move the supply curve up or down.

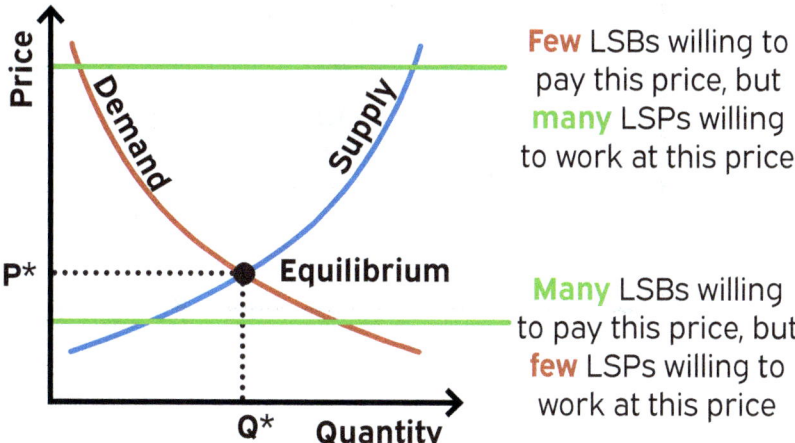

Figure 8: Price equilibrium is at the point where demand and supply curves meet.

This means that, in theory at least, every time a new LSB approaches the industry to buy language services, it increases overall demand and shifts the demand curve to the right. However, when a new LSP opens for business, the supply curves to the right, increasing overall supply. The effect is pretty miniscule, due to the decentralization and diversity of the industry, but this can add up over time. The industry is growing as a whole. More and more customers are demanding language services and so the demand curve is constantly shifting. The reason the market prices remain somewhat stable is because the supply curve is shifting along with it, increasing supply at the same rate as the increase in demand.

This relationship between demand and supply is not coincidental, nor is it simultaneous. First, the demand increases as more and more LSBs are purchasing language services. The effect of this is that the market price (P) point goes up.

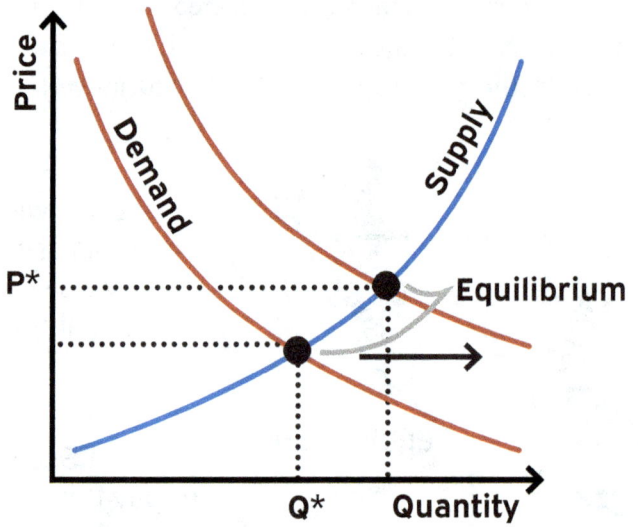

Figure 9: As LSBs buy more, the demand curve shifts to the right. This increases the equilibrium price in the industry. Higher prices mean more new entrants will be tempted to enter the market.

The increased market price makes the industry more profitable for everybody as existing companies now have more bargaining power and can charge higher rates. But it also makes the industry more attractive to new entrants. The more profitable the industry is, the more likely new entrants will be motivated to open for business.

Perhaps you are working for an LSP currently and are dreaming of one day going out on your own and starting a new business. You have done the calculations based on the market and determine that you could only make 20% margins if you were to start a new business today. On the other hand, you like the comfort and security of your nice salaried position. You decide that the potential risk is not worth the potential reward, and you keep your salaried job. However, some time goes by and increasing demand in the industry has caused the market price to increase. You re-run your calculations and determine that you could possibly make a 35% margin if you were to start your own business, which is much more appetizing to you. You quit your day job, rent some office space in your parent's garage, and you go into business for yourself. This means the industry as a whole now has one more new entrant supplying service to meet the demand.

Congratulations, you have just shifted the supply curve. This shift in the supply chain drives price (and therefore, margins) back down towards the original market price. This is how industry forces work to constantly be driving the price towards the equilibrium point and also how increasing profitability actually increases the threat of new entrants to the industry.

The Jell-O Effect

To summarize our discussion on the threat of new entrants, we would like to introduce you to a concept that we call "the Jell-O effect". This is not an official market influencer. Nor does Michael Porter ever mention it in his Five Market Forces Model. We've coined this term ourselves. It is a useful tool for demonstrating how the language services industry is affected by new entrants. The Jell-O effect describes how and why the industry is under constant threat of new entrants as a result of the extremely low barriers to entry.

What happens when you squeeze a block of Jell-O? Think about this question, as we attempt to explain.

When other industries like automotive or tech are "squeezed", companies go out of business or are acquired. The big companies get bigger and the small companies get bought or go out of business. People lose their jobs and the labor market is suddenly flooded with qualified and experienced talent. This means that other companies now get their pick of some very experienced people. It also means that unfortunately some of those people affected will be looking for employment for quite some time, since there are just not enough jobs available for all of them. Perhaps some of them find work outside the industry. Others may contemplate the idea of going into business for themselves and starting their own company, but most give up on this plan because of the high startup costs. So when most industries are squeezed, the result is like squeezing a tin can. You end up with a smaller, different shaped version of the original.

What happens when the language services industry is squeezed? Well, mostly the same thing. People get laid off. People look for new jobs. People dream of going into business for themselves. But because of the very low barrier to entry in the industry, those people who are contemplating starting their own business actually have the power to do so

Furthermore, people don't tend to leave the language services industry. Perhaps it is because they feel their skills are so specialized or perhaps it is because they just love what they do, but it is very rare for an established industry veteran to go seek employment in another industry. When the language services industry is squeezed, you don't end up with a smaller version than the original, like a tin can, you end up with a mess. Just like if you were to squeeze a block of Jell-O. Sliding through your sticky fingers and onto the table.

Whenever the industry is squeezed, it doesn't condense, it spreads. When one company goes down in flames, it means three more will rise from the ashes. This is the Jell-O effect and it is why there will never be a shortage of new entrants in this industry.

Threat of Substitutes

At first glance, you may wondering what the difference is between the threat of new entrants and the threat of substitutes. After all, if a new competitor enters the market, then of course there is a risk that the client may substitute your services with theirs, right? This is why it is important to draw a clear line between the threat of new entrants, the threat of substitutes, and standard industry rivalry.

Here, the term "substitutes" is being used to describe products or services that exist outside of an industry's standard set of services or products, which can relatively easily be used to replace those services or products. When a new entrant comes into the industry, they could steal some of your business away from you, but they won't be taking any of that business outside of the industry as a whole. The delicious pie of the industry is still the same size, but your slice just got a little bit smaller. The same is true if one of your existing competitors takes business from you. However, when customers start to switch from your services to substitutes from outside of the industry, it not only decreases your slice of the pie, but it also decreases the size of the whole pie. This drives down prices and margins for you and your competitors.

Driving this threat of substitutes is a number of factors that should be taken into account when analyzing the industry, including (but certainly not limited to) the following:

- Availability and number of substitutes
- Quality and nature of product/service
- Pricing of substitutes
- Cost associated with switching (substituting)
- Difficulty/Ease of substitution
- Buyer behavior (willingness to substitute)

Our Market Influencer evaluation will focus on two different types of substitutes: substitutes for translation and substitutes for Core LSP Functions. Translation is the ultimate service that is being provided through the language services value chain, but we need to keep in mind that the majority of players in this value chain are LSPs and don't actually provide translation. Instead, LSPs add value through the Core Functions of project management, vendor management, and sales. Only the translators actually add value through the act of translation, so they are at greatest risk of being replaced by substitutes for translation.

If translation is replaced by a substitute service like machine translation (MT), for example, there is still an opportunity for an LSP to add value by managing the machine translation process, much like they previously managed the manual translation process. However, if their Core Functions are substituted, there is no opportunity for the LSP to retain their relevancy in the value chain. Workflow automation can replace project management. Crowdsourcing platforms can replace traditional vendor management.

Availability and Number of Substitutes

The first factor affecting the threat of substitutes in the language services industry is the availability of substitutes. This provides us with the opportunity to take a closer look at some (if not all) of the more commonly discussed substitutes. Fortunately for us (and for you, who has to read through all of these), there are not many. Generally, if LSBs want to localize their products and services to better compete in the global marketplace, they must employ LSPs for the necessary adaptation, translation, interpretation, and other services.

Companies either translate their content or they don't. It is tempting to say that "do nothing" is the biggest competitor to the LSP. Translation can be expensive, and some customers just aren't ready to open their wallets. We can't even begin to tell you how many times we have seen a potential customer decide not to buy language services simply because they chose instead to do nothing. However, "doing nothing" is not technically a true substitution because in order for it to be a true substitution it would have to effectively achieve the same results as the original service.

Substitution Threats
- Crowdsourcing
- Automation
- Machine Translation
- No translation
- Artificial intelligence

This is not to say, though, that there are zero options for the price-sensitive LSB who wants to reach a global audience without forking over the big bucks. There are certainly ways to strategically cut some corners and we discuss several of these in this section.

In the previous section on the threat of new entrants, we focused on LSPs and CLPs because it is a threat that affects players on the vendor side of the value chain. For the following section on substitution, we focus our examples less on LSPs and more on LSBs, because the decision to use substitute services lies solely on the client side.

Machine Translation

Earlier in the book, we (begrudgingly) touched on language technology providers (LTPs) and acknowledged that they play a very important role within the industry. One category of LTPs is machine translation (MT) providers, who develop complex software and artificial intelligence to translate content into multiple languages without any human interaction at all.

Remember that in the first chapter we identified the language services industry as any and all business related to helping clients (language services buyers) adapt or create content, products or services in order to better compete in the global marketplace. LTPs undisputedly fit nicely into this definition. So, MT may not technically be a true substitute at the industry level. This having been said, MT providers represent a very small fraction of the industry as a whole. And a big chunk of the development in this area is happening on the client side because only obscenely large companies like Microsoft and Google have truckloads of money needed to perform research and development in MT.

For these reasons, we will be looking at MT as a substitute service that threatens the larger localization services industry. We understand that those reading this book from the perspective of a language technology specialist may be frustrated to not be included. However, they can take pride in the fact that they are disrupting the foundations of the language services industry to the point where people like us are rewriting the book to account for it.

The reality for LSPs and translators is that MT has not quite reached the point where it can be a full substitute for human-generated translation. MT has been around for a long time and LSPs and translators are still making a lot of money. Perhaps the day will come when machines are able to replace human translators, but when that day comes, we will have larger problems to worry about, as we huddle in our bunkers plotting our resistance against our robot overlords.

For now, MT can be thought of as a productivity tool that can be used in specific situations to increase the output of traditional translation supply chains. Translators have adapted to this new technology by becoming expert MT consultants, or offering machine translation post-editing (MTPE) services. Meanwhile, LSPs have adapted by simply adopting it into their project management toolkit and using it to add value.

IKEAzation

For those of you who have been living in a cave for the last several decades, let us please take a moment to get you up to speed. If you are already aware, please feel free to skip the next few paragraphs. IKEA is a global home furnishing warehouse store. The first IKEA opened for business in 1957 and since then they expanded into other Scandinavian countries before moving on to Switzerland and Germany, then to the rest of Europe, and ultimately to the rest of the world. As of the time of writing this, IKEA operates over 300 stores in over 41 countries worldwide.

All of IKEA's products come unassembled. Not because IKEA doesn't know how to assemble furniture, but rather because this is all part of the grand strategy. This allows IKEA to keep logistics costs low and also creates a whole new class of customer – the buyer without a truck. If you were to buy a new bed from a typical furniture store, you would need access to a truck or a moving van to bring it home, or you would need to pay extra for delivery. If you were to buy the same bed from IKEA, you would walk out of the store with a compact box full of components that could easily be tied to the top of your Skoda or even dragged onto a public bus back to your apartment.

Truly, they are one of the most sophisticated global players in the home furnishings industry, competing in local markets that used to be completely dominated by domestic companies. While there are many interesting case studies to be taken from IKEA's globalization strategy, the one we are most interested in today is how they localize their documentation. Each of those unassembled pieces of particle board need to be constructed at home by the customer, which means each product comes with a set of instructions.

Typically, installation, assembly, and maintenance instructions constitute about 90% of content that is localized by a company, which essentially means that it also represents about 90% of the company's costs for localization. That is a lot of expense. However, from the LSP's perspective, it is a lot of revenue! Ikea eliminates this cost completely by creating instruction manuals with only pictures and not a single word to translate. They have effectively substituted localization with cartoons.

IKEA did not invent this strategy; it has been around for ages. Next time you are in an airplane, take a look at the passenger safety card in the seat back pocket. You will notice that there are no complicated instructions in multiple languages, only pictures. How many times have you ever accidentally gone into the wrong gender bathroom in a foreign country because you couldn't understand the signs on the doors? Never, because this information is almost always conveyed through pictures, not writing. IKEAzation is a viable substitute for translation for any company looking to convey very important information in a way that is understood by anybody, regardless of language.

Crowdsourcing

Crowdsourcing has been very much in vogue in the language services industry for a number of years now. The idea is that rather than pay high-priced translators to provide translations, companies could just let "the crowd" translate for free. Facebook is perhaps the most influential LSB that popularized this method. They had so many passionate users around the world that they could simply allow these users to provide their translations for free. This also meant that the translations were being provided by scores of amateur translators with very little quality control.

Crowdsourcing is not a substitute for translation. After all, the whole concept of crowdsourcing is that there are "real" translators working on the content, even if they are unvetted amateurs. Essentially, crowdsourcing is a substitute service for the Core Function of vendor Management as it removes distance between content and translators. When one of the three Core Functions is essentially eliminated, LSPs are not able to add as much value and therefore lose their competitive advantage.

Fortunately for LSPs, crowdsourcing seems to have decreased in popularity in recent years. After the excitement and hype wore off, people began to view crowdsourcing much like they view MT – a useful tool to increase productivity in a very specific situation, but perhaps not the industry disruptor that everybody thought it would be.

Process Automation

Process automation threatens to replace many aspects of the project management Core Function. When we talk about automation, we could easily be talking about a number of things. There are project management tools that increase productivity, therefore reducing the amount of project management services needed. There are also fully automated solutions that seek to cut project managers out of the workflow.

We delve deeper into our discussion on project management automation in Part 2 of this book. Here, we suffice it to say that the threat of process automation acting as a potential substitute is real, though not as worrisome as some may think. LSBs would like nothing better than to cut out the need for project management completely from the language services value chain. A fully automated process has long been the sought after Holy Grail of the industry. For

A FULLY AUTOMATED PROCESS HAS LONG BEEN THE SOUGHT AFTER HOLY GRAIL OF THE INDUSTRY.

now, let's just say that process automation, much like machine translation and crowdsourcing, can be a very effective tool when used properly in specific situations. It is still, however, a long way off from completely eliminating the need for project management for most companies.

Smart LSPs have embraced this trend towards automation. Technology Support Activities are established to enable project managers to add more value with fewer resources. This allows LSPs to stay relevant and competitive by providing even more value through their project management Core Function than they would be able to without the aid of automation.

Quality and Nature of Product/Service

Some products and services are easily interchangeable. Others, not.

The human race's ability to so effectively communicate with each other is what separates us from the animals. There is nothing that can fully replace language. Nothing. Not even really well drawn IKEA cartoons. Of course, some people who come back from a year abroad or from a weekend silent meditation retreat talk about how verbal and written language just serves to separate us and puts our minds into boxes and that real communication is the language of the heart. Hogwash. If you don't speak English and you call 911 in an emergency, you are going to be very grateful when an interpreter comes on the line.

What we are trying to say here is that language, by its very nature, does not have any fully effective substitutes readily available. We use language to build relationships, to learn more about the world around us, to convince others to agree with us, and for practically every other activity that makes humans, well, human. This is true for the language services industry more than almost any other industry in the world.

Virtually any other product or service in the world can be

replaced by a substitute. Perhaps not easily, but it can be done. Take away your iPhone, and you will spend more time on your computer. Take away Renato's car, and he'll substitute it by taking the bus. Take away Tucker's coffee, and he'll substitute it with a sharp knife in your throat. All of these changes would suck horribly, but we would survive. However, if you take away language, we lose our relationships, our identities, and so much more of what makes us humans. So it is safe to say that language itself is not in danger of being replaced by a substitute.

However, this doesn't mean that other Core Functions cannot be substituted. Project management, vendor management, and sales can be automated to a certain extent, as we touched on above. So far, attempts to fully substitute any of these Core Functions have proved to be less than fully effective. Years ago, MT was supposed to replace translators. It hasn't. Recently, crowdsourcing platforms were going to replace the need for vendor management. Last time we checked, this hasn't happened either. Companies that offer to automate and simplify the language services value chain are nothing more than an attempt to cut out the sales function and the value it adds by educating and consulting with their clients. As of today, nobody has been able to replace the unique value of human consulting in the industry.

At the end of the day, the language services industry is still relationship-driven. Nobody has yet been able to find a suitable substitute for human relationships.

Pricing of Substitutes

If the pricing of substitute products or services in any given market is lower than that of the original products and services, the likelihood of customers shifting their attention to the substitutes increases. If the pricing of substitutes is higher, then it decreases the risk of customers switching. The substitute would only be worth considering if there was a risk that market prices may change to the point where the substitute's price may decrease.

Think about how many biodiesel vehicles you see driving down the road. Not many, right? Biodiesel is technically a feasible substitute for regular diesel. However, biodiesel is currently about 150% more expensive than regular diesel. So if you make your money selling regular diesel, you may acknowledge that biodiesel is a potential threat because if it drops in price (or if regular diesel increases in price), you suddenly face a situation where your customers are going to switch over to biodiesel.

This factor of pricing is by far the number one driver that increases the threat of substitutes in the localization industry. As we have discussed already, there are few, if any, good reasons other than price for an LSB to look for alternatives to language services, so the decision is almost always driven by price.

The pricing of MT, for example, can be anywhere from practically free to thousands of dollars. This really depends on the level of sophistication you are looking for from your MT engines. There are a number of publicly available MT options that you could technically start using immediately, but you may not get very good results. If you have some budget to spend, then you would develop or license customized MT engines that could be specifically trained with your brand-specific content so as to get better results. Generally speaking though, even when an LSB partners with an MT provider to license customized engines, the greatest costs are incurred up front. After the initial set up, the monthly subscription and maintenance fees are nominal – much cheaper than paying for the content to be translated by an LSP. Typically the return on investment for MT comes quickly and is quite profound.

Substitute Switching Costs

Costs associated with switching are sometimes different than the overall price of substitutes. Above, we used the example of the higher prices of biodiesel compared to traditional fuel deterring customers from making the switch. This works as an example when talking about pricing because typically there are no conversion costs to switch your vehicle from diesel to biodiesel. If you have a diesel engine, you can substitute biodiesel tomorrow without having to make any additional modifications to your vehicle.

What would happen, though, if you wanted to convert your vehicle to run on natural gas? Generally, natural gas is much cheaper than biodiesel, so there is a clear cost advantage here. However, before you can substitute natural gas for diesel, you would first need to invest in making the proper modifications to your vehicle's engines. These modifications are costly and represent the cost associated with substitution.

The same is true when it comes to substitutes for language services. As mentioned for MT, the overall price is heavy on the initial setup costs to develop and train the MT engines. Other initial costs could be restructuring or rewriting your content to be optimized for MT processing, which will also take time and money.

The costs associated with switching to IKEAzation are likewise something to consider. If your content already exists in a written format, then you will have to go back to the drawing board to redesign all of your content. Depending on your organization, this could be a very long and costly endeavor, as you will have to pay content creators to recreate everything with this in mind.

For any automation or tooling seeking to replace project management or vendor management, we see similar results.

Generally, the costs up front are pretty high because it takes time and expertise to develop the solution. Once the solution is developed, then the overall costs should drop. In theory, the automation should pay for itself. Clients will perform a detailed RoI (Return on Investment) analysis before making any decisions. If the potential savings are more than the costs, then it may make sense for them to substitute. For the LSP, this means that there is always the incentive to provide more value at lower costs, so as to make sure it never becomes a cost-effective strategy for their customers to make the switch.

Difficulty/Ease of Substitution

So far, we have made the point that there is really no full replacement for language as a means of effective communication. If not, then maybe we have been too subtle in our opinions. However, there are certainly specific scenarios where it would make a lot of sense to save some budget by substituting. Just with the examples that we have looked at of MT and IKEAzation, it seems that these should be relatively easy to implement. So what, you may ask, are LSBs waiting for?

To answer this question, we have to get into a small discussion about how localization is typically managed by LSBs. To put it mildly, many LSBs don't have a single goddamned clue what they are doing when it comes to localization. Some are better than others, and some are downright brilliant, sure, but as a general rule, they are lost.

To support this controversial and incendiary claim, we would like to point to the mere existence of the "localization department" within LSBs. The fact that there is a clear distinction between localization and the rest of the company speaks volumes. Localization is treated as an afterthought—a problem to be solved, and so it is delegated to the lowly localization team so that the real experts in the company can focus on the company's core competencies, whatever those may be. Now, personally, we like localization departments. They have paid us a lot of money over the years. But unfortunately they are typically completely cut off from the rest of the company and unsupported. Furthermore, in many new companies, the localization department doesn't even exist yet, and the task of translation is just another thing added to the plate of an already busy marketing manager. But we digress...

Let's say, for example, that a very experienced and capable LSB localization manager wants to cut localization costs by implementing MT strategy and substituting more instructional graphics for heavy text. She has done her research. She feels that by using illustrations more effectively, total word count can be decreased by 40%. Furthermore, she knows that if the remaining content is formatted in a certain way and written in a certain style, the results from MT would be of acceptable quality. However, currently all of the content she is being asked to localize is poorly written and completely unstructured, making it unfeasible to implement a cost-saving MT strategy.

At this point, this is where our poor localization manager realizes her complete inability to affect organizational change outside of her own department. Her idea could be brilliant and could save the company thousands or even millions of dollars, but she is unable to get the organizational buy-in from key stakeholders within her company to execute. In theory, this substitution would be very easy to implement. However, when our localization manager tries to bring about the necessary changes to implement this new strategy, she is faced with insurmountable internal resistance.

Historically speaking, the above example is not only common, it is the norm. Until recently, it has been very rare in this industry for an LSB to have a culture and setup that facilitates and streamlines localization from start to finish. This is because most companies have designed themselves to focus on their home market. Only after they are successful in their home market do they start thinking about localization, but by then it is too late. There are of course exceptions to this rule. Recently, we have seen an encouraging number of startups starting from day one with an international strategy and building localization best practices into their entire workflow.

Willingness to Substitute and Influence of the LSP

Buyers are usually more than eager to move forward with a substitute service. Sometimes this motivation is just to save some money. Sometimes it is because they are trying to be innovative. Sometimes, it is simply out of ignorance of how language works and they aren't aware of any of the potential risks of not investing in proper localization. If the LSP is not prepared to have a conversation with these clients and educate them, they could lose a potential opportunity.

An LSP, particularly those working in its sales Core Function, needs to have an intimate knowledge of substitute services. If a client asks them about it, they can act as a trusted advisor, lending them their knowledge and expertise and possibly even steering them away from a decision that would not be good for them in the long term. At the very least, an LSP needs to know about substitute services because if a client decides to switch, the LSP must have a strategy to fit into these new plans.

If a customer decides to use MT, many times there is not much that can be done to change their mind. An unprepared LSP could lose the whole account. A prepared LSP, on the other hand, could consult with the customer and let them know the dangers of using raw MT without any human review. They may still lose the translation business from that client, and revenue will certainly drop, but perhaps they can add value by managing the MT process or providing low cost machine translation post-editing (MTPE) services. By being prepared, an LSP can turn a sure disaster into a possible opportunity.

Let's say you are working for an exciting startup that produces a hot new smartphone app. You have had great success in your home market and now want to go global. In order to do this, you will need to localize several different types of content. Firstly, you need to localize the app itself. Secondly, you need to localize the online support articles and frequently asked questions (FAQ). To advertise your app in new markets, you will also need to localize some of your existing marketing content. And lastly, there is legal content such as the end user license agreement (EULA) and terms and conditions.

Rather than bundling all of this up and sending over to an LSP for translation, it would be wise to take a look and see if each of these four content types need to have the same level of service applied. Your actual app user interface (UI), of course, needs to be superb quality, so additional testing will be in order. But if your analytics data shows that your online help content only gets a couple dozen visitors per month, you can ask yourself, "Does my online help content really need to be perfect, or will MT suffice here?" Legal content may need to be completely rewritten in each market, depending on the local regulatory requirements. Your marketing content is going to be your first impression on potential customers, so this needs to be really high quality and MT could damage your brand image. These are decisions that need to be made by each LSB, so no standard answer to these questions is available.

An LSB who takes the time to analyze its content types will identify different quality levels for each, and then assign a process accordingly. Content that doesn't need to be high quality could be machine translated. Since documentation is typically much more content than the actual product, this means that the savings can represent a very large portion of your localization budget. A simple analysis may look something like the chart on page 77.

The above analysis helps determine the buyer's willingness to substitute translation for MT. If the required quality level is high for all categories, then their willingness to use MT is very low. However, if there are no quality concerns and they have no budget for localization, their willingness to substitute is very high.

Component	Description	Quality Level	Process
App Strings	Directly affects UX	Very High	Human translation followed by additional testing
Online Help Content	Low visibility	Low	Machine translation with post editing
Marketing Content	First impression on potential new customers	High	Human translation by specialized marketing translators
Legal Content	Required documentation from local regulatory and legal agencies	Medium	New content creation in each local market

Remember that translation is bought per word. If you can be more selective about the amount of content you are localizing, then the number of words you are paying to localize will drop accordingly.

Another way to drop word count is with IKEAzation. You don't even need to go to the extreme of IKEA, cutting out all of their words and replacing them with cartoons. If you can simply author content in a way that relies more heavily on graphics to explain concepts, then you reduce your total word count. It is important to note here, though, that this means the graphics need to be simple, without any text, and easily understood. This applies not only to your documentation, but also to your UI.

Let's look at a practical example. Let's assume that we want to localize the below user interface into German. An LSP is going to charge us US $0.25 per word to localize. You want to calculate how much it will cost to have a screen of UI translated and are looking at two different ways of formatting your UI, as in the example provided.

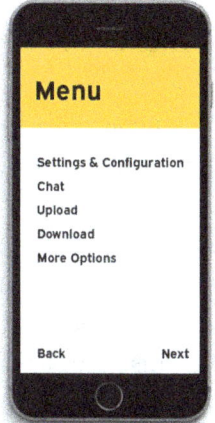 

These two screens have the exact same functionality, but one has literally 1,000% more text to translate. The one on the left is going to cost more to be translated and may also lead to more problems from character encoding, text expansion, and God only knows what else. The screen on the right replaces the text with simple, easy-to-understand pictures that don't even need to be touched in order to be ready for most markets, saving 90% of localization costs!

If the LSB decides to implement this strategy, it all but eliminates the need for translation. Does this, then, mean that the LSP is out of work? Not necessarily! Let's face it: most likely the client did not come up with this idea on their own. They got the idea from somewhere else. This means that they are open to consulting. An LSP that is able to effectively coach their clients on language services best practices will always be in demand. Sure, they may end up coaching themselves out of their old job of providing translations. Still, they are evolving their service offerings to make sure they still have some influence and continue to add value to the language services value chain, even if it is through completely different services.

Bargaining Power of Customers

Anybody who has worked in the language services industry for more than a day or two has had to deal with the bargaining power of customers. Hell, anybody who has ever had to work customer services to put themselves through college has had to deal with this. Perhaps you are working as a CLP, paying the bills by taking freelance jobs for an LSP. Or perhaps you are working for an MMLSP and your customer base includes Microsoft, Apple, and the rest of the Global Illuminati. Regardless of your position on the value chain or whom you count amongst your customers, the hard truth will always be that while the customer most certainly is not always right, it doesn't much matter because they are the ones that are going to help you keep the lights on.

It is tempting to fall into the trap of crying foul and complaining about how unfairly the customers treat the poor little LSPs. The customer is being unreasonable. The customer is cheating me. The customer poisoned my dog and stole my girlfriend. We've heard (and said) it all at different points in our careers. But such conversations aren't so much pointless as they are damaging— damaging to your own position and power to fight back against the very injustices against which you are rallying. The more time we spend denying or arguing against the current state of the industry, the less objectively we can accurately analyze our position in it and take steps to ensure our own personal success.

This is by far the most powerful force at play within the language services industry and certainly the one that most people come up against most often. Some of the factors that affect the bargaining power of customers in the industry are:

- Availability of information
- Costs of switching vendors
- Buyer concentration and size of industry
- Price sensitivity of buyer

- Competition in industry
- Availability of substitutes (see threat of substitutes)

In this section, we discuss the bargaining power of customers in the localization industry and what effect this has on companies. In the next section, we talk about the bargaining power of suppliers.

In order to have a meaningful discussion of both, we will have to frame the conversation in a consistent way. So, we structure our conversation for the next two sections around a typical MLSP that is providing language services directly to an LSB and contracting directly with SLSPs and CLPs to perform the work.

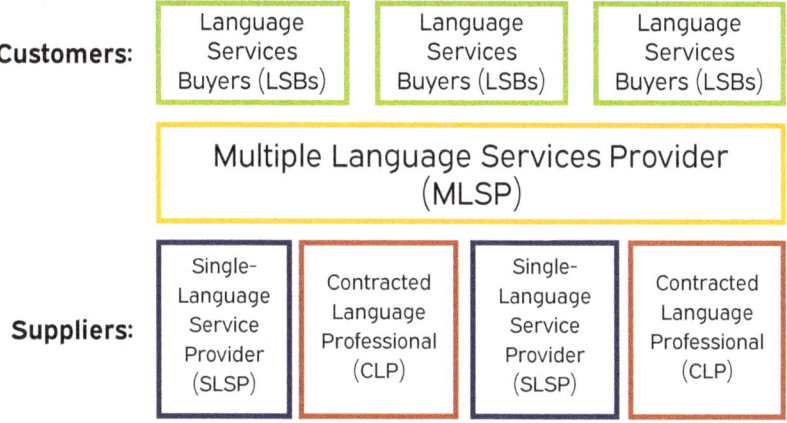

Figure 10: A typical MLSP provides services to LSBs and contracts with SLSPs and CLPs to perform the work.

However, this analysis could be done for any company in the supply chain. You could perform the analysis from the point of the CLP, defining your customers as the various LSPs you work for. If you are a localization manager working for an LSB, you could define your customers as your internal stakeholders requesting localization. Remember that the point of the Market Influencer evaluation is to not look at the industry as a whole so much as it is to look at a specific company's position within that industry and how that is affected by the five forces.

Now that we have properly framed the analysis, let's take a look at some of the factors driving up the bargaining power of customers from the perspective of the MLSP.

Availability of Information

Information, as we have already discussed (see Operating with Low Information), may not be publicly accessible from outside the industry, or even from inside the industry, for that matter. However, the industry is small and close-knit, meaning that gossip flies. If you have ever lived in a small town where everybody knows what truck you drive, then you know exactly what we are talking about. So while there are few officially published channels for industry information, the information is readily available to those with the experience and connections to know where to look for it. This unofficial availability of information increases the awareness and therefore the bargaining power of buyers.

At first glance there seems to be plenty of information available from LSPs' websites. Keep in mind, though, that this is marketing material, not unbiased information. It is important to take a look at the source of any information and ask yourself, "What are they trying to sell me?" Mostly, they are trying to sell you their services, and are only presenting the information that they have handpicked to make themselves look most attractive. That fascinating blog you just read on how in the near future all translators will be working exclusively from smartphones? That's probably from a company that just developed a new technology for this and is trying to peddle their wares. South American LSPs will publish articles and blogs about the importance of adapting Spanish for different Latin American countries, while European LSPs will counter with blogs about how money would be better spent on European languages.

As with so many aspects of the language services industry, it depends on who you know. The relationships you build in this industry are the best tool for figuring out the real information that will help you make better decisions. You would do well to join industry associations and attend networking events to build your circle of trusted colleagues. These will be your best source of information that you can rely upon as you try to navigate the industry.

So how does this strange environment affect the customer's buying power? Simple. The more information that customers have at their disposal, the higher their bargaining power. Think about it. Would you want your customers to have access to all of your competitor's prices? Of course not! Because they could use this information to drive down your prices, or even worse, they could just leave you to go work with one of your cheaper competitors.

Unfortunately for LSPs, whether or not your customers are getting quality information is not really important. For example, let's say one of your customers attends an industry conference and hears a presentation from your competitor about how the future of translation is crowdsourcing. It just so happens that this competitor specializes in setting up crowdsourced solutions and is merely trying to steal your customer. But that doesn't matter to your customer. They are going to act on this information. For this reason, you would be wise to learn which industry events your customers are going to so you can be there as well.

Buyer Concentration and Size of Industry

The language services industry is huge. There are thousands of buyers and hundreds of thousands of suppliers. So any analysis at the industry level of buyer concentration will be very short. Simply put, this is not an industry with a high level of buyer concentration. There are thousands of buyers and more buyers are entering the market every day.

This is not to say, though, that we simply overlook the factor of buyer concentration. We have discussed so far how most LSPs work hard to carve out a niche for themselves in the industry, so they are not trying to be all things to all customers. This is why we see some LSPs specializing in technology, while others specialize in legal or marketing translations. Yet others provide staffing or interpretation services.

Let's look at an MLSP specializing in providing full service translation to technology companies in Silicon Valley. The number of startups in California is growing daily and is not expected to change. At first glance, this would seem like the land of milk and honey for any LSP. But our MLSP has a certain customer profile they like to adhere to. They have decided that they need to pursue companies that are translating into 10 or more languages and have a budget of at least $500,000 per year to spend on translation services. This is not uncommon in the industry. As different LSPs occupy different segments, each one is free to define their target customers.

By sticking to this customer profile, our MLSP is cleverly applying some of the concepts we have already discussed above. They are able to leverage considerable economies of scale, invest in integrating their technology with that of their clients to increase stickiness, and increase their own bargaining power with their vendors. Our LSP is effectively positioning itself so as to reduce the threat of new entrants and substitutions. However, by so doing, it is actually increasing the bargaining power of its customers by artificially limiting the number of potential customers that fit into their acceptable customer profile.

This goes back to our supply and demand curves. The more customers there are wanting to purchase your services, it shifts the demand curve and works to drive up market prices, giving our LSP more bargaining power to negotiate rates with those customers. By putting limitations on the types of customers they are willing to work with, our LSP is artificially constraining the size of their potential market and decreasing the number of LSBs they can sell to. Fewer LSBs means higher buyer concentration, which works to drive down your margins.

Cost of Switching Vendors

Switching vendors can be expensive, which can lead to decreased bargaining power of customers. This may sound familiar because we've already discussed this in the section on substitution costs. If an LSB were to switch to a new LSP, what would be the costs incurred in order to affect this change? It may be upfront financial costs, though commonly the costs are harder to define or are intangible.

The most reliable determiners of switching costs are the level of integration between customer and supplier systems and the level of outsourcing between the customer and the supplier.

Level of Integration

When we have discussed integration before, we have done so largely in the context of tooling integration. For example, an LSP may have developed a tool that syncs up with the client's content management system, streamlining the localization process. If the customer wants to change suppliers, then they would have to build a new tool that does the same thing with their new supplier. Often it is a huge headache for a customer to do this, so they will stay with an existing LSP far longer than they would like to. From an LSP standpoint, integrating systems to increase relationship stickiness is a powerful strategy to increase your bargaining power in relationship to the client's. But now let's take a look at why this may not be enough.

Customer stickiness does not mean that LSPs can take their customers for granted. In theory, the level of stickiness is proportional to the level of integration you have with a customer. But reality may be different from theory. If a customer is happy with your services, they will stay. If a customer has decided to change, they are going to change, and there is not much you can do about it that isn't just postponing the inevitable.

Level of Outsourcing

Integration between service providers and customers generally means that processes typically done by the buyer are eliminated and replaced with automation. This adds value to the customers because it means their work is decreased and therefore they reduce their internal costs. Another way to decrease the buyers' work is to simply shift that work over to the supplier side by outsourcing.

If you think about it, there is always a minimum level of outsourcing that happens when an LSB engages with an LSP. The LSB is paying the LSP to outsource the translation and associated management processes. So when we are looking at the LSB-LSP relationship, it is not a matter of whether the LSB chooses to outsource, but rather how much they outsource. This decision is made by each LSB based on a number of factors such as budget, ability to outsource, nature of services being outsourced, internal structure, company values, privacy and confidentiality concerns, and comfort level with the idea of outsourcing.

As an LSP, it is always the goal to get more and more work from your existing clients. As we discuss in later chapters, business is grown not just by acquiring new clients, but also by growing your existing accounts. Existing accounts grow if the LSB experiences an increase in volume, of course, but an enterprising LSP is not usually content to wait for their clients to send them more work. A growth-oriented LSP is always looking for ways they can add additional value for their clients by taking on additional services.

Some LSBs prefer to keep the majority of their localization process in-house so they can retain a tighter control over the process. Sometimes this is the best route, especially if they have a very experienced and capable localization department (note:

every LSB thinks they have a good localization department). If you are an LSP working with such a client, your goal here would be to build trust with that client and slowly shift more and more key components over to your team. Before you know it, the client has outsourced almost all functions relating to localization. When this happens, the LSP is now the expert and knows more about the LSB's localized products and services than they do. All of this means that it will be very costly for the LSB to switch suppliers because they have literally no clue of where to even begin.

There are a lot tools and other intellectual property that is developed to run a localization program. Some of this IP is rightfully owned by the LSB, such as any translation memories (TMs), glossaries, and internal tools. However, perhaps the current LSP is the only one that knows how to properly segment the content in order to maximize the efficiency of those TMs, or perhaps they have developed their own tools that augment (or even fix) the client's proprietary tools.

All too often, when a client develops a tool for localization, it will require about three additional tools to be developed on the vendor side. At best, this is to augment existing features or to make them compatible with vendor side tools, and at worst, this is required to compensate for the gross inadequacies of the client side tool.

This is why business savvy LSBs will write into their contracts specific processes to be followed in case of a transition in order to hold the LSPs accountable during this phase.

Usually the incoming and outgoing LSPs play nice with each other in a common display of cowardice that is not often seen in other industries. LSPs will bend over backwards to help a client that has just fired them

GENERALLY, LSPs PLAY NICE EVEN AFTER THEY ARE FIRED. YOU DON'T BITE THE HAND THAT FEEDS YOU IN THIS INDUSTRY.

because, in their mind, this is how they protect their information and leave the door open for more table scraps in the future. Also they know something that the client doesn't: Chances are high that the new vendor will fail.

Price Sensitivity of Buyer

Price sensitivity refers to the emphasis that a client places on price in relationship to other factors when making decisions. Let's say you arrive in London and you need to search for an app to navigate the subway system. You find one in the app store and realize they want to charge you $0.99 to download it. Do you do it? Probably not. Here you are, one click away from having all the information you need to safely navigate one of the most unforgiving mass transit systems in the world, but you refuse to pay even a dollar for it.

This is because when it comes to apps, buyers are notoriously price-sensitive. After refusing to download the app, you may then hop in a taxicab to get to where you need to go. Do you research to find the cheapest taxi company and understand all of the costs before getting into the cab? Probably not. This is because as a taxi customer, you are price-insensitive. This example illustrates how the same person can have different price sensitivities depending on the product or service being purchased. Language services buyers are no different.

Price sensitivity in the language services industry is something that is hard to discuss in a general way, because it varies largely with different LSBs. We've worked with LSBs that have money to literally burn if they wanted to. We've also worked with LSBs with budgets so tight they must make hard decisions about which services they can buy and which may have to get deprioritized until next year's budget. As a general industry trend, though, localization managers are being asked to do "more with less" and this is not expected to change any time soon. Sometimes LSBs are able to come up with ideas on how this is going to happen, but usually their grand plan consists of going to suppliers and announcing that now they have to do more with less.

We could write a whole book only on price sensitivity, given the many different forces at play here. For now, though, it is enough to say that price sensitivity is high, and because we are operating in a high competition industry, this high price sensitivity works to increase the bargaining power of the customer.

Competition in Industry and Availability of Substitutes

Substitutes have been discussed earlier in great detail, and we look closer at industry competition later. For now it is enough to note that increased competition and availability of substitutes can both lead to a higher bargaining power of customers.

Bargaining Power of Suppliers

Now it is time to turn our eyes downstream and take a look at the bargaining power that suppliers bring to the table. For many LSPs, this will be a refreshing change of pace, moving the discussion from one of relative impotence to one of power. CLPs may get upset by this section, as it basically outlines how your customers can work to push your prices down, which is surely an existing source of frustration for you. CLPs generally do not have a supply chain. They are the supply chain. Regardless, we think the topics covered in this section will be insightful for anybody, not just vendor managers.

There are many factors affecting the bargaining power of suppliers. In this section, we take a closer look at some of them, as listed below.

- Degree of differentiation
- Impact of inputs on cost and differentiation
- Presence of substitute inputs
- Supplier concentration

- Employee solidarity (e.g. labor unions)
- Competition with suppliers

Degree of Differentiation

Differentiation here refers to the degree to which a product or service can be distinguished to make it stand out from products or services offered by competitors. Differentiation adds unique value that cannot be easily reproduced by other companies, thus providing a competitive advantage. When it comes to LSPs, they must differentiate based on their ability to execute Core Functions.

Let's say that an MLSP contracts with two different types of suppliers to perform the language services requested by their customers. For some projects, they contract directly with CLPs and for some others they contract through smaller SLSPs. At the end of the day, what our MLSP is purchasing from both of these suppliers is the same: translations. But it pays the SLSPs a higher rate because of the higher degree of differentiation to their services through their Core Functions. Another word for differentiation here is value. Differentiation is how LSPs add value to the language services value chain.

CLPs, on the other hand, provide only translations, and there is no additional project management, vendor management, or consulting. If CLPs have been working on the projects for a long time, they can create a level of differentiation for themselves in that they have more experience with the work than others. However, an experienced MLSP works to reduce this power by carefully managing knowledge through standard methods like using translation memories, glossaries, and style guides. It also thoroughly documents any project-specific information so that it can easily be shared with new CLPs should they need to be replaced.

The SLSPs, on the other hand, provide project management

support to make sure projects are delivered on time. They manage schedules so that when translators are out sick or on vacation there are backup translators already available. They provide a single point of contact to the
MLSP to cut down the time needed to manage multiple CLPs. Each of these additional services gives the SLSP another way to provide more value and therefore a higher degree of differentiation to their service offering.

Higher value service offerings in turn increase bargaining power. Our MLSP will have a harder time replacing high value SLSPs. For most MLSPs in this situation, the decision to work with SLSPs is a calculated trade-off. MLSPs are perfectly happy to sacrifice bargaining power for the added value that the SLSPs bring to the table. Any MLSP who has ever had to work directly with hundreds of translators knows this very well.

Impact of Inputs on Cost and Differentiation

Market prices in the industry are set by the supply and demand curve and are very stable over any short period of time. It is very hard for suppliers to have any impact on overall costs. If our MLSP is to decrease their total costs so that they can enjoy a higher margin (or perhaps lower their prices for their clients), they must cut those costs that don't impact their suppliers. While suppliers may make up the majority of costs for an MLSP, their rates remain quite stable and have very little impact on total cost fluctuations.

When our MLSP goes to the negotiation table with their suppliers, generally everybody knows what the market price is. This effectively takes away the suppliers' ability to increase their prices, especially in the absence of any significant differentiation of their services. So in this regard the suppliers' bargaining power is actually decreased. On the other hand, though, it takes away any power the MLSP has to drive prices down below the current market price. The MLSP knows just as well as the supplier that they are not going to get a better rate if they talk to other suppliers. If another supplier is able to give a better rate, it is probably because they are cutting corners in other areas and it will end up costing them the same in the long run.

Supplier Solidarity

When we discuss solidarity in the context of the Market Influencer evaluation for other industries, we would refer to organized labor forces. They are able to combine their influence and increase their collective bargaining power with their employers or customers. However, in the highly decentralized and competitive language services industry, it would be hard to imagine that any such supplier solidarity could exist. Still, it would be a mistake to disregard supplier solidarity completely when performing market analysis. So, let's look at the types of solidarity that we see in the language services industry, starting with the effect of governmental and cultural view on labor. We then look at how communities have organically organized within the industry as well as some examples of formal organization.

Cultural Attitudes

Different cultures have different views on work and labor, and these views are often codified into law by local governmental labor agencies. Because specific services in the industry are linked directly to location, this can lead to an unintended yet powerful form of solidarity among suppliers.

Anybody who has ever managed Chinese translations is surely familiar with the Chinese New Year. We are all so used to it that we hardly ever stop to think about how big of an irregularity this is, but let's take a moment to appreciate the significance here. Every year, translators, project managers, engineers, and all other types of suppliers in China basically tell their customers that they will be performing no work for a whole week. In China. This is a country that is more than willing to work 24 hours a day for the remainder of the year. Under normal circumstances, they may as well just copy their resignation letters into their out-of-office reply before leaving for such a holiday. But because this is a cultural norm that is also supported by the local government, Chinese suppliers have an extremely high degree of bargaining power and everybody else in the world has to just accept this and work around it.

Likewise, any LSP project manager who has ever tried to get a French translator to work over the weekend has surely been rejected more than a few times. For another language, this may lead the project manager to fire the translator and search for somebody with a more "American" work ethic. However, it is common knowledge that French culture lends itself to a certain degree of solidarity on the subject of overtime hours. Although they are not organizing intentionally, they nonetheless stand united on this point, giving them the bargaining power to "negotiate" working hours, and vacation time that would not be granted to a less galvanized labor force.

Organic Communities

Because most translations happen at the CLP level, one would think that there would be very little collaboration between individual translators, especially since the market is so competitive with many different suppliers competing with one another. However, there are in fact a number of resources available for CLPs that allow them to share their experience and organize communities with each other. These have largely developed organically and are not often incredibly sophisticated, but they serve to provide a level of organization that would otherwise not be available to CLPs.

One feature available to members of online communities is the ability to rate the different LSPs and LSBs they have contracted with. CLPs can create an account, log in, and make comments on their experience working with different companies for other CLPs to read. It's basically like Yelp, but for the language services industry. If you are a CLP who has been contacted by an LSP for a big job, your most likely first step would be to go check their score. You may read that they have a bad reputation and don't pay their suppliers on time, or that they are very unorganized and waste your time or don't follow through on their commitments to suppliers. This information leads to informed decisions about whether or not to engage with them and if so, what rates to charge. If they have a poor reputation then you may still choose to engage with them, but will charge higher rates in order to cover the additional risk. Likewise, if a company has a great relationship and always pays on time, you may lower your rates to be a little more competitive.

These organic communities are even more effective depending on the size of your market. For a market with a lot of supply, like English to Spanish translation, it is very difficult for such communities to have any influence on the industry as a whole. However, for a market with a very small number of qualified translators, organization is much easier and vastly more powerful. Let's say you are an MLSP that needs to translate medical documents into Haitian Creole and that there are only three translators in the world qualified to perform such translations. If this is the case, it is almost guaranteed that they know each other. Hell, they probably attended each other's weddings. While this may not be an official labor union, it may as well be, since they are very organized and you have no choice but to work with them.

These principles hold true especially for location-dependent work. Nowadays, translation occurs globally, with files being sent all over the globe for completion. However, translation is just one form of language services. It is important to remember that interpreting is still a very local market. There are some projects that can be completed by an over-the-phone interpreter. But the vast majority of interpreting work is done in person and it can be expensive to pay travel expenses to send interpreters wherever they are needed. Since some interpretation jobs require multiple interpreters, it is not uncommon that in any given city, the interpreters have worked together at the same jobs and so they mostly all know each other. And if they know each other, then we can guarantee that they are sharing notes on the best and the worst companies to work for, so it is very important to stay off their "worst" list.

While such online and offline communities are a far cry from being organized labor unions, they are nonetheless powerful. They put transparency of information into the hands of the CLPs and other suppliers and therefore increase their bargaining power. For an MLSP that relies heavily on engagement with either other LSPs or CLPs, it is absolutely imperative that you are aware of the risk of disregarding such organic communities. It may be rare that such communities actually refuse work, or "go on strike", but they can powerfully affect your brand equity. Many LSPs have been baffled as to why their supplier costs seem to be slowly increasing over time, only to realize too late it is because their suppliers are all telling each other online about how they should not work with you.

Formalized Unionization

There are very few formalized labor unions in the language services industry. The low barrier to entry and high level of competition all but ensures that effective unions will never be able to take hold. When unions do exist, they are either for specialized work, such as governmental translations that require certain skills and certifications or for services that overlap with other industries where unionization is more common. Take, for instance, voiceover artists who are part of actors' guilds and unions from the larger entertainment industry.

Competition with Suppliers

Whether or not companies directly compete with their suppliers is another factor that affects the bargaining power of suppliers. Essentially, this refers to whether or not it is feasible for a supplier to start selling to their customer's customer. Cut out the middleman, in other words. If this is possible, then it can increase the bargaining power of the suppliers.

Consider how Apple works with various retailers to sell their products. In this example, Apple is the supplier for the retailers. Now we're sure these retailers maintain a pretty high level of bargaining power with most of their suppliers. But in their relationship with Apple, who do you think wears the pants? Apple, of course. Surely, this is due in part to the high demand for Apple's highly differentiated products, but it is also because Apple has the ability to cut any retailer out of the process completely. Apple sells its products online and in their own stores, meaning that they are competing with their own customer for market share. This direct competition means that Apple holds a disproportionate amount of the bargaining power in its relationship with its customers.

We have already demonstrated how low the barriers to entry are in the language services industry and how it can be relatively easy for LSPs to grow and expand their services. Sometimes this means that LSPs who work for other, larger LSPs (that is, an SLSP working for an MLSP) will start expanding into services provided by their clients. In other words, they start expanding into the same niche as their customers.

Once this happens, then the SLSP doesn't need their customer as much and may start to think they can cut them out and work directly with their clients. Just how MLSPs will sometimes cut out the SLSP and work directly with CLPs, it is also possible for the SLSP to cut out the MLSP and work directly with the LSB. In such a scenario where the supplier is able to compete in the same niche as the customer, it should go without saying that the supplier holds a much greater bargaining power.

You may be wondering how much this actually happens. Well, although it is entirely theoretically possible, the reality is that it doesn't happen too often. LSPs are usually content to stay within their lane and not invite additional competition by venturing outside of their niche, which brings us nicely into our next conversation on industry rivalry.

Industry Rivalry

Industry rivalry influences the market but is in turn also highly influenced by the other four Market Influencers. It is important to keep in mind here that industry rivalry does not just correspond to the number of competitors, but also to the way in which these competitors interact with each other.

As you may have guessed, the language services industry is a little... different in this regard. The industry seems to be driven by a number of unwritten rules that are taken for granted by industry insiders, but can be absolutely baffling to an outsider. These unwritten rules are influenced by a number of factors:

- LSP concentration ratio
- Innovation and competitive advantage
- Marketing expenditure
- Competitive strategy
- Transparency and the small-town effect

In the following sections, we dive deeper into each of these factors to see how they influence rivalry in the language services industry.

LSP Concentration Ratio

The most influential factor affecting competition is the LSP concentration ratio. It is a measure of how concentrated the total amount of business is with a small number of firms. Fortunately, we don't have to reinvent the wheel here and define a way to measure this ourselves. We can rely on a useful tool that is widely used to measure firm concentration ratio: the Herfindahl-Hirschman Index (HHI).

The Herfindahl–Hirschman index (HHI) is a way of measuring concentration among players in an industry. It is calculated by squaring each player's total market share and then adding all of these together. A high number will mean that the industry is very concentrated. The higher the number, the closer the market is to a monopoly. A lower number indicates that the market is more decentralized and therefore more competitive. HHI is a well-known measure for market concentration and is used by private businesses, as well as government and regulatory agencies to measure market concentration. For example, the Antitrust Division of the Justice Department uses HHI to decide whether or not to approve mergers that could potentially limit competition in an industry.

The language services industry has an HHI index of 67. This seems pretty high, right? Well, we may have forgotten to mention that the HHI Index is on a scale of 1 to 10,000. Generally speaking, a score from 1,500 to 2,500 is considered to be a moderately concentrated market, while any score above 2,500 is considered to be a concentrated market.

The language services industry is not fragmented. It is completely pulverized. You would be hard-pressed to find a less concentrated market. If you take the top 20 players in the industry, they represent less than 5% of the whole market for language services. Compare this, for example, to the personal computer industry, in which only the top six companies make up almost 80% of the total market share. There is no one single player or group of players that comes anywhere close to controlling the language services industry.

Even in an industry where mergers and acquisitions are a pretty common occurrence, the market has only gotten more decentralized with the passage of time. Low barriers of entry, the Jell-O effect, and continuously decreasing costs of running an international business are some factors that ensure sustained healthy competition. The top companies can grow and acquire competitors, but they will never catch up with the ever-increasing demand in the industry, and we will continue to see small LSPs entering the market and ensuring that the LSP concentration remains low.

What this means for LSPs is that there will always be competition. Always. Most large LSPs have accepted this and have long ago given up any dreams of overtaking the market. In the language services industry, LSPs do not compete at the industry level. Considering the level of competition in the industry as a whole, that would be madness. LSPs compete at the niche level. By carefully defining their niche, LSPs are able to shrink the overwhelming amount of competition to a more manageable level.

Innovation and Competitive Advantage

To discuss how LSPs compete with each other through innovation, we must first describe the landscape in which we find ourselves and the prevailing attitudes towards innovation in the industry.

It seems that any LSP that is able to scrape together a small R&D budget immediately starts dreaming on how they are going to revolutionize the industry with their innovative new technology or process. Go to any localization conference around the world and listen to the frothy mouthed presenters swearing up and down that they're going to disrupt the industry with their controversial and ambitious new ideas. Like many other industries, we worship faithfully at the altar of Almighty Innovation. The problem is that the language services industry has proven itself to be horribly equipped to actually innovate in any meaningful way. Still, this doesn't stop anybody from talking about it.

Those of us who have been around for a little while recognize these boasts for what they are, which is nothing more than delusions of grandeur. Some actually believe that they are going to change the industry by bringing new innovation. These are the True Believers. There are others, though, that realize deep down that it is all just a show. They need to talk about innovation in order to get the attention of the clients and to build the perception that they are innovative. The only thing more important than actually innovating, so it is thought, is that other people think that you are innovating.

One of the worst things that can happen to an LSP is to be labeled an unbeliever. Customers don't want to work with LSPs that are happy with the status quo. They want to work with LSPs that are driving innovation in the industry. They want to work with the True Believers.

And so it is in this environment where we find that not only must we play along, but we must also not be caught speaking ill of any innovation, no matter how absurd and no matter what the source. (Somebody has found a way to reduce costs by training cybernetically enhanced catfish to process XML files? Awesome!

Tell me more!) What this does is to create an echo chamber in the industry, with nobody willing to speak out and express skepticism. This is especially strange because it means that even LSPs that are directly competing with each other are too afraid to speak ill of their competitor's technology out of fear of being labeled an unbeliever. You can surely see how this affects industry rivalry.

Let's say your primary competitor gives a presentation at a conference showing their automated no-touch crowdsource-supported neural machine translation platform, which of course is in the cloud and optimized for mobile for some goddamned reason. (Note: We made that example up, but it is not too farfetched compared to some of the ridiculous stuff we have heard at conferences. We could provide real life examples, but would like to avoid libel lawsuits as much as possible). Now they end their presentation and ask for questions from the audience. What you want to do is raise your hand and scream at the top of your lungs: "Bullshiiiiiiiiiiiiit!" But you don't. There are poor gullible clients present and they are believing every word that your competitor just said. So you say nothing.

Months later, you are talking to your client. They mention they saw this presentation and ask you what you think. This is your opportunity. You've been working with this client for years and have built a high level of trust with them. You should let them know they can't trust a word of what they heard. But you don't. Instead, you claim that you found the presentation inspiring and that your company is also working on something similar, and you're very excited about it. All hail Innovation!

This is the environment in the language services industry. In some ways, it could be considered highly competitive, with each LSP shouting that they have the best and most innovative tools and processes. In other ways, it is not competitive at all, because most of those proprietary technologies are at worst completely useless or at best on par with or only marginally better than third party software available to all LSPs.

The reality is that two players drive real innovation in the industry: customers and startups. Most established LSPs do not drive innovation because they just cannot afford to. They are focused on growing their business and hitting margin targets and therefore are reluctant to make any real investment into research and development. Customers drive innovation because they can afford to. Hell, if Amazon can afford a space program, we think they can afford to throw a few dollars towards developing MT engines. If LSPs are lucky, the customer will invite them to participate in this process.

Startups, on the other hand, drive innovation because they have to. By their very nature, startup companies do not have the millions of dollars in R&D budget that customers do, but they have something that most customers don't: flexibility and fresh ideas. Those massive customers that can afford to spend millions on innovation are unwieldy giants. Typically, by the time they get to that size, they have lost most if not all of their organizational agility and ability to follow through on fresh and innovative ideas. Startups are smaller, more agile, and more passionate, and so while they may not have the same budget, they drive innovation if for no other reason than because they must.

Marketing Expenditure

Typically in the language services industry, there are not many high cost marketing channels. Of course, every company has a website. That website may host various marketing materials such as blogs, videos, or webinars. Marketing departments may craft email campaigns targeted to their target customers, but typically most marketing content is pretty generic in order to appeal to the widest possible audience and rarely contains any life-changing new information. As a result, it is usually pretty inexpensive to roll out. The point is, nobody is taking out a full-page ad in the New York Times or buying airtime during the Olympics.

Such marketing channels certainly add value in lead generation, but for language services, the majority of the sales and marketing happens in person. This is an industry of relationships. The vast majority of lead generation and new client acquisition happens in person at conferences. For this reason, the majority of most LSPs' marketing budgets goes into travel expenses to make sure their companies are well represented at these events.

Attendance at conferences such as TAUS and Localization World (Loc World) is pretty much mandatory if an LSP wants to stay relevant in the industry. Every conference that you do not attend means not only that you are missing out on the opportunity to build relationships with potential new clients, but it also means that your existing clients are there alone. And, we can guarantee that your competitors are inviting them out to dinner in your absence. The key thing to understand is that it is absolutely critical for the LSP to make this investment into building relationships through in-person contact with clients.

When we look at the Core Functions in Part 2, we will discuss in much greater detail how the sales Core Function contributes to the value chain through relationship-building and education. Localization can be incredibly complex and many customers, as we so eloquently put it earlier, have no idea what the hell they are doing. Salespersons add value by consulting and educating these customers so that they understand what they are buying and why they are buying it. It is absolutely critical for LSPs to invest in their sales Core Function.

At this point, we feel it may be necessary to point out an observation we have made through our years in the industry. We shouldn't have to point this out, but unfortunately we do. Here goes. The companies that grow the fastest are the companies

that invest the most in sales and marketing and employ the most salespersons. Makes sense, right? Well, even though this seems like common sense, it needs to be reiterated because in the language services industry there are a lot of companies that for some reason do not understand this simple concept. Sometimes, this is by design. It makes sense, for example, to not grow too fast or by pursuing the wrong type of clients, and every LSP is free to follow their own growth strategy. However, if growth is your goal, then it may be time to hire more salespersons, send them off to build relationships, and continue investment into sales and marketing to sustain growth.

Competitive Strategy

One of the things that strikes outsiders when they attend language industry events is that competitors, subcontractors, and freelance translators are friendly and collaborative. There are very few bitter rivalries, no Coke versus Pepsi feuds. Mostly this is because there is so much diversification in the industry. Sure, the industry is highly fragmented, but there are so many unique niches that most LSPs don't compete with each other. In fact, they may even be incentivized to cooperate with each other to a certain extent.

When we speak at conferences or have workshops, we bring hundreds of people from dozens of companies together in the same room. Even with a large amount of people in attendance, very seldom do we find people who compete directly with one another. There is so much diversification, true competition is rare. It is more likely that you are going to collaborate with people in the room than compete with them.

In other industries, companies compete against each other as if they were two soccer teams trying to win a match. It is very clear who the competition is and the single goal is to make sure you score more goals than they do. In the language services industry, you are still somewhat competing against the opposing team, but they are not the true opponents. The real opponents are baseball, hockey, and basketball. While you are trying to beat the opposing team, you are also working together to steal customers away from other sports. Sometimes we need to collaborate with the companies we think are our competitors and other times we need to compete with companies we think are collaborators.

About 10 years ago, Renato gave the closing remarks at a conference in Cordoba, Argentina. As Renato tells the story, there were probably 800 people in the room (which is to say, there were probably 400). The attendees in the room were from different Argentinian LSPs. As Renato remembers, they were very shy at the conference and he could tell that they did not collaborate with each other outside of seeing each other at conferences. They saw each other as competitors.

Renato raised a few eyebrows when he told them that they were thinking small. They have the most advanced education system in the Americas. They have high English proficiency. They have the smartest, most well-educated people (he probably also commented on the good looks of their women). He told them their competition is not the person sitting next to them, but the guy in Mexico, Uruguay, or Panama, who speak Spanish and are competing directly with all of them.

In the industry, we know that the Argentine translator is better educated than the rest of Latin America. If you disagree, then just remember, he was speaking to a very specific audience. Their goal should be to work together to create a brand. They should start branding all of their translations as "Translated in Argentina". Rather than compete with each other, they should collaborate so that they, as a group, could better compete with their true competitors in the industry. You will know that your brand is successful when somebody in Peru starts branding their translations "Translated in Argentina".

Well, they didn't take his advice, at least not right away. However, what they did do years later was create an open association that provides a local community for Argentinian LSPs. They can cooperate and support each other through networking and "Translated in Argentina" conferences. They have decided to stop competing and start collaborating.

The spirit of rivalry in the language services industry is essentially one of "coopetition". Even when you are competing with somebody directly, it makes sense to cooperate to a certain extent. It is completely plausible that CEOs of rival companies are competing for the same multimillion-dollar contract one week and then speaking on the same panel at an industry conference the next week. When two LSPs are both working for the same LSB, they work together. They try to impress the client with their spirit of cooperation, rather than competition.

LSPs that have been around for a while know full well about the concept of coopetition, even if they have never used that specific term.

Transparency and the Small-Town Effect

In many ways, working in this industry is like living in a small town. This can often be intimidating to industry outsiders, because anybody who has watched a few old Western movies has an idea of how outsiders are treated.

Sometimes it seems like everybody knows each other, for better or worse. It is an industry where mini celebrities are born and people brag about who they know and how long they have known them. Growing up in a small town is much the same. Even if you don't know everybody personally, chances are that you know of them or you know somebody else who does.

Working in language services is like dating in a small town.

Industry Rivalry

There is a limited pool of companies to work for and let's just say that there is a large degree of "cross pollination" going on. It seems that everybody has worked with everybody else at some point in their career. If they haven't, then they know somebody who has. And people are more than willing to talk about their past experiences.

So, it is particularly important to make sure you keep your nose clean in this industry. In a small town, secrets only last until the next church potluck and then the whole town knows about them. Likewise in the language services industry, you will not have secrets. Period. You may be able to fool industry outsiders for a while, but not for long.

It also means that there is a certain insular nature to it all. You don't sit down and write a resume. You get a job because your uncle manages the Pizza Hut on Main Street. Language services are all about who you know and, more importantly, the impression you make on them. What you think of the small-town effect is largely a matter of perception. Some use words like networking, others use words like nepotism. Some say insular, other say close-knit. It is not our point here to be preachy in calling attention to this. It is our point to point out a prevalent phenomenon in the industry and to let you think what you want of it.

How does this affect industry rivalry? Well, like in a small town, people talk, and your standing in the community is your greatest asset. So, LSPs are always careful to make sure they maintain a good reputation, not just with customers but with everybody.

Defining Your Niche

This brings us to the conclusion of the Market Influencer evaluation. To recap, we have looked at the five Market Influencers: the threat of new entrants, the threat of substitutes, the bargaining power of buyers, the bargaining power of suppliers, and industry rivalry. Each of these Influencers is further influenced by a number of different factors at play within the industry, and we looked closely at many of these.

Now that you have a working knowledge of the five Market Influencers, it is time for you to use this information. If you are thinking of starting a new company, look at the industry as a whole, utilizing the concepts outlined in this section, and plan how you would differentiate your product. Where are the risks? Where are the opportunities? How can you set your new business up so as to add the most possible value?

For those of our readers who are already working in language services, the Market Influencer evaluation is especially useful because you have a real life scenario that you can analyze. Does your LSP have a plan to deal with the potential threat of new entrants? What steps are you taking to educate your clients about substitute products? Are you taking full advantage of your position in the market so as to minimize the bargaining power of your supply chain and your customers?

The result of the Market Influencer evaluation is to basically stop and take stock of where you are, identify risks and opportunities, and then plan your course forward. In the next sections, we bring the conversation down to the LSP level. We discuss how to set up the infrastructure of your LSP to maintain the Support Activities necessary to add

the maximum amount of value through Core Functions. Smart LSP owners don't organize their company in a vacuum. They rely heavily on the insights gained from the Market Influencer evaluation to make sure they are best equipped to compete in their niche.

Part 2: Into Action

The Seven Support Activities

Alright. We survived Part 1. Thanks for hanging in there with us. That was a long one, we know. But it was necessary. The Market Evaluation provides the information and insight that we need to start looking closely at your own position in the market, which is what this section empowers you to do. Here, we focus less on the industry and more on individual companies.

As you already know, Support Activities do not directly add value. They only enable the Core Functions to add value. Support Activities, in the context of the General Theory of the Translation Company, are defined as activities carried out by an LSP to provide infrastructure, direction, or resources to enable and optimize an LSP's ability to add value through the Core Functions.

In the diagram, the Support Activities are depicted in a circle separating the Market Influencers and the Core Functions. This is very much how they act in practice as well. In a highly functional LSP, the Support Activities are designed in such a way to build a bridge between market forces and operational teams within the LSP.

This section examines the seven Support Activities of the LSP:

1. Management
2. Structure
3. Finance
4. Culture
5. Facilities/HR
6. Technology
7. Quality Assurance

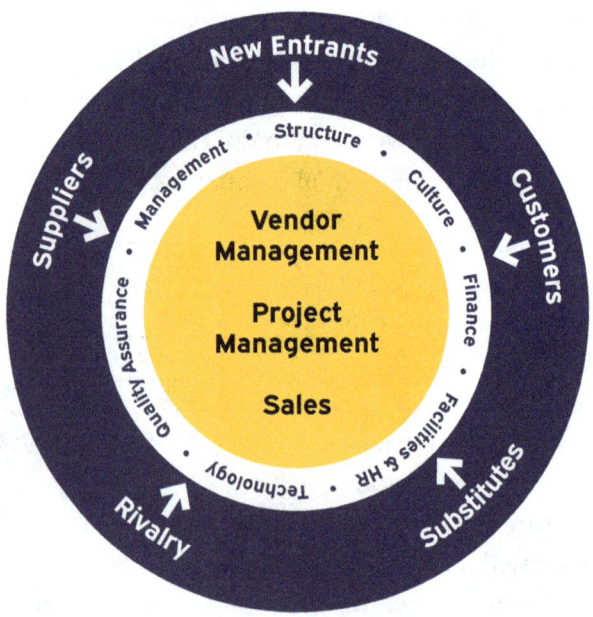

Figure 11: Support Activities act as bridges between market forces and operational teams within an LSP.

These Support Activities serve to enable or optimize the Core Functions by providing strategy and vision, economies of scale, growth, productivity, global manpower, efficiency, and consistency respectively.

When discussing Support Activities, we talk about the nuts and bolts of the LSP. Companies vary in size, location, languages, services, and a thousand other characteristics. There are almost as many different types of LSPs in the language services industry as there are LSPs, and each company brings something unique to the table. We will do our best to approach the following chapter in such a way that we are being as inclusive as possible so that any industry player will be able to take away something relevant to them. Out of necessity, though, we have to make certain generalizations. The easiest way to do this will be to frame the discussion around a typical MMLSP, since this is clearly the largest and potentially most complicated player in the book. Principles that apply to the MMLSP will mostly apply to smaller LSPs, only reduced in scale.

Figure 12: Support Activities provide the services that enable Core Functions.

Keep in mind that our goal here is not to teach you how to manage an LSP. That is for you to figure out. There is no "right" way to organize an LSP. Your business structure will depend on how you have defined your niche in the industry and is going to (hopefully) be set up so as to optimize your ability to add value to your customers.

Management

The key function of any management team is to provide strategy and vision for the rest of the company. The first step of developing the strategy and vision is the Market Influencer evaluation. By analyzing the market, the leadership of an LSP can formulate a clear plan on how to get from where they are currently at to where they want to be. Oftentimes this vision is codified officially into a company's vision or mission Statement (note: these are basically the same thing).

We haven't seen it yet but one day we would love to see an honest company unveil their new corporate mission statement that is just a bunch of green dollar signs followed by smiley face emojis. Or perhaps a Vision Statement that includes the CEO's dream of one day owning a vacation home in Malta. Because at the end of the day, a company's job is to make money, especially for its owners, right? While that may be true, the management owes it to their team to provide a more detailed picture of where they are going (the vision) and a roadmap on how they are going to get there (the strategy).

This can be done by writing a mission statement, vision statement, or defining company goals or best practices. Management should be very open about their strategy on how they plan to grow the business or enter new markets, communicating this down the chain of command and ensuring that the entire company is on board with the vision.

Remember that an LSP adds value only through the Core Functions, which are not typically carried out by senior managers. The managers' jobs are to enable and optimize the Core Functions. It doesn't matter how aligned the management team is with each other, if they aren't aligned with the teams carrying out the Core Functions of vendor management, project management and sales.

A company's employees, specifically project managers and salespersons, are the company's strongest channels to the clients. If the thought of being out of touch with employee's needs does not concern you too much, then you should think about what this means for your relationship with your clients. Firstly, disgruntled employees provide lower levels of customer services. Secondly, customers don't typically pick up the phone and call the CEO to explain their needs. Customers funnel this communication through their LSP project managers and salespersons, because that is the level where trust is being built daily.

IF SENIOR MANAGERS ARE NOT AWARE OF THE NEEDS OF THEIR EMPLOYEES, THEN I GUARANTEE YOU THAT THOSE EMPLOYEES ARE NOT AWARE OF THE NEEDS OF THE MANAGER.

If communication channels are in place for the customer's feedback to be properly escalated to the management team, then senior managers will find that they are not only out of touch with their employee's needs, but also with the needs of their customers. On the bright side, once a company loses touch with their customers, the problem usually solves itself, as they will soon find that they have a significantly fewer number of customers they must manage!

This book is not presuming to make a judgment call on how each LSP should structure their management team or communication.

Each company is unique and so each company must find a method that works for them. What is important is that you are aware of the challenges so that, regardless of the decision, your LSP's vision and strategy can be effectively communicated to all of your global team members and that you are working as one team towards a common goal.

Culture

One of the most important things that senior management of any organization can do is to set the culture for the company. The quality of the culture that you have as a company will affect all aspects of your business, from employee retention to customer satisfaction, to profitability. Most noticeably, a company's culture is directly related to employee productivity. A company with a healthy culture will enjoy highly productive team members. A company with a toxic culture will have unhappy and unproductive employees.

This can be especially true for a language services company because of the nature of the industry. When we looked at the small town effect during the Market Influencer evaluation, we learned that in the language services industry everybody seems to know everybody else. Which means that companies that don't care about their culture are going to have a hard time finding quality people to work for them, and since a company is nothing more than the people it is made up of, all aspects of their business will suffer.

Culture comes from the top. No exceptions. You may have heard some people claim that culture grows organically from all levels of an organization, but that is simply not true. If culture did in fact seem to grow organically within an organization, then that growth was allowed or encouraged by the senior management.

Employees at all levels of a company are constantly looking to their managers to take cues on how they should act, whom they should trust, and what they should do. The way their managers treat them ends up being the way they treat their direct reports, all the way down the chain of command. Therefore, culture necessarily comes from the top. This is not to say, though, that it comes in the form of an announcement or a mandate. Culture is cultivated through modeled behavior from senior managers and specifically the CEO. If you want to know more about a company culture, learn more about their CEO. That will be the best indicator of what to expect for any given company.

Pick from any of the core values that most companies (not just LSPs) will list: accountability, respect, hard work, etc. Let's go with respect. The website is updated to advertise to the world that one of the company's core values is respect. PowerPoint presentations are given and articles are written for the company newsletter. The sales team tells every new client that ours is a culture of respect and we put a premium on treating one another with decency. However, let's say that the CEO engages in behavior contrary to this value, frequently belittling his VPs in front of their colleagues, or gossiping about them behind their back. Those VPs will take their cues from him and that is how they will treat their department heads, who will then treat their project managers the same.

Culture needs to be actively maintained. It takes work, it

takes time, and it takes (gasp) budget to make sure that you are maintaining control over your company's culture. Growing and maintaining a healthy and productive company culture is a lot like growing and maintaining a garden.

Every summer, Tucker likes to grow a vegetable garden. Living in the Pacific Northwest, this is not always an easy accomplishment. Tucker is ultimately responsible for the end result of the garden, but he has to work within the confines of his situation. Tucker can't just force the garden to grow the way he wants to. Let's say he decides that his garden is going to be full of watermelons and okra. However, this would be a foolish decision because those crops simply do not grow in the Pacific Northwest and at the end of the growing season he will be sorely disappointed. If, on the other hand, Tucker decides he doesn't want to plant anything or maintain his garden beds, at the end of the growing season, there will be plenty of plants, but mostly they will be weeds and things that were not intended to grow. But let's say that Tucker plants kale, beets, and spinach, all crops that grow well in that region. This would be a smart decision, as it is something that is most likely to turn out favorably. But Tucker is only a gardener and there are many other factors such as weather, length of the growing season, and especially that god damned mole that ate up all of his squash plants last year. He can do his best to influence the garden and make sure it is set up to succeed. But he also needs to be flexible and recognize that while he can plant the garden and maintain it, he cannot make it grow. The garden grows on its own.

Senior managers in a localization company are responsible for creating culture in the same way that Tucker is responsible for growing his garden. They must make important decisions about how they would like to steer their company's culture. These decisions must be based on the constraints of their local cultures. This is done through modeling the desired corporate culture, as employees will mirror what they see from their managers, not what they are told. One last time: Culture comes from the top.

Structure

As a company grows, the organization becomes increasingly difficult to manage. As a rule, the maximum number of people any manager should have reporting to him is around seven. If a manager has any more than this, it quickly becomes more than she can control and she is not able to manage effectively. The same holds true for an LSP, especially if a manager has to manage remote employees in different time zones.

Example: Structured by Location

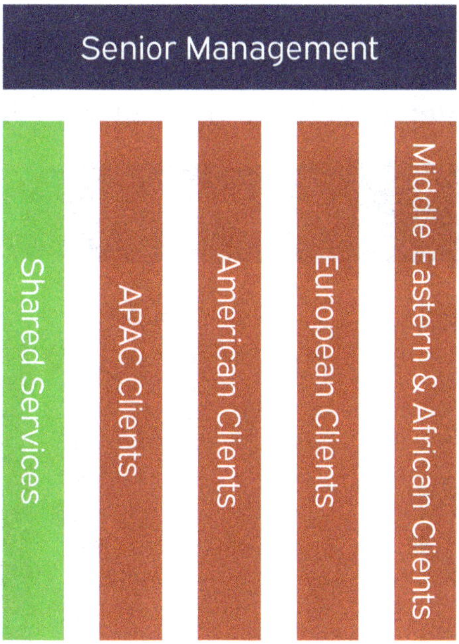

Figure 13: An LSP's structure by location.

You have probably noticed a theme by now that there are really not any set formulas that apply to all LSPs in the industry. This holds true when defining a reporting structure for your company, too. How your company is structured will depend very much on your specific situation. This is not to say that an organization's structure and hierarchy should be arbitrary or that it is not important. It is critical to define an organizational structure that enables you to add the most possible value through your Core Functions. The primary way that you can better enable your Core Functions is by creating an organizational structure that best allows you to take advantage of economies of scale as you grow your business.

One of the key factors to help you determine how to organize your company will be the type of your customers and how you deliver services to your customers. Your organizational structure needs to support your delivery model to allow for the best, most efficient services to meet your client needs. Here is where a close examination of the Market Influencers for your specific niche can provide excellent insight into how you can structure your teams.

Example: Structured by Industry (Vertical)

[Diagram: Senior Management at top, with columns below: Shared Services, Technology Clients, Life Sciences Clients, Entertainment Clients, Manufacturing Clients]

Figure 14: An LSP's structure by vertical.

Are you managing a highly automated transactional process with a very high volume? Because of the nature of the automations taking place, you can likely operate with far fewer project managers, which means you will need fewer managers to oversee them. This

Structure

may also mean that internal costs are less of a concern and you can afford to have your teams centralized rather than offshoring work to lower cost locations and choosing to send only translation work to linguists offshore.

Or perhaps your customers are such that they send steady and predictable volumes of work, but demand a more personal touch with more project management support and linguists on demand during business hours. In this case, you will need more (and better) project managers and you may also consider having an in-house linguist model in order to maintain tighter control over your translation teams.

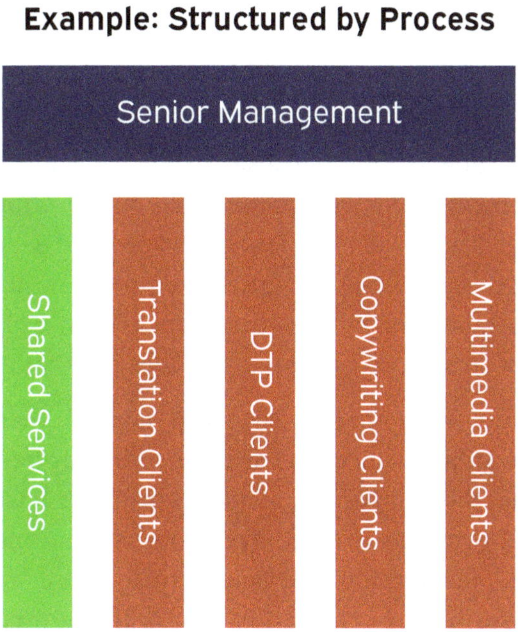

Example: Structured by Process

Senior Management				
Shared Services	Translation Clients	DTP Clients	Copywriting Clients	Multimedia Clients

Figure 15: An LSP's structure by process.

For all LSPs, but especially larger MLSPs, it is important to look at where there may be economies of scale to leverage by combining teams working on similar clients. This could mean that you consolidate clients into different teams based on any number of factors. It could be that a specialized team manages all clients using a certain process or buying a specific service. By grouping these into a single division, you can ensure that expertise about the processes is cultivated. Or you could define team specializations around managing market verticals. This could be a good decision for verticals where a lot of expertise or special certifications are needed, such as for life sciences projects or government contracts.

Note an important distinction we made here that it is important to group experience needed to manage different clients or types of work, not to translate those types of work. Remember that an LSP is not a translation company, it is a services company. If your company wins a contract to manage translation of large pharmaceutical legal contracts for a government agency, you are going to be using the same translators as your competitor would have if they had won the contract instead.

The value that you add is through managing this process. So what is important for your purposes is the institutional knowledge about the process for managing such work. Grouping work together that is not similar to manage will not lead to economies of scale, but if certain clients or verticals require specialized skills to manage the translation process, then it makes sense to consolidate these groups so as to take advantage of these economies of scale.

Frequently, a company's structure doesn't seem to make much sense at first glance. This is not necessarily because of any mistakes that the company has made, but rather it is usually just the way that company evolved over time as their business grew. For example, (everything else being equal) there is no need to have separate business units for clients in the manufacturing industry versus clients in the technology industry. Surely, different translators should be employed for each of these, but from a project management perspective, the process is pretty much the same. If there are not different tools, credentials (such as government security clearance or ISO certification) or project management skills needed, it probably doesn't need to be organized into a separate unit.

Finance

Finance is one of the key support services that an LSP needs to have in order to enable continued success and growth. As with the other Support Activities, finance does not actually add value to the process of executing and delivering language services for the customers. However, the finance team creates an environment where the teams carrying out the Core Functions can successfully do their jobs by making sure they have the resources to grow.

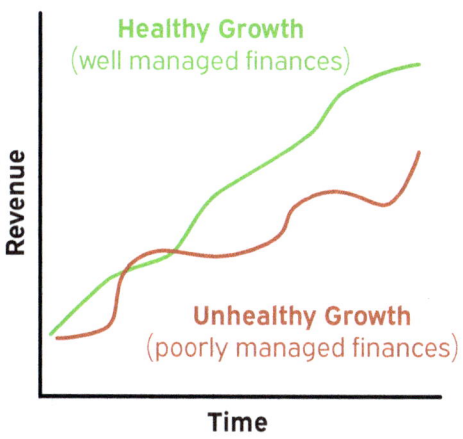

Growth requires investment and can be downright expensive. The finance Support Activity manages the books to make sure there is sufficient capital to invest in growth activities while still maintaining a healthy profit margin. If an LSP is publicly traded or beholden to external investors, then the finance function becomes even more important. Public companies live or die on their financial health as reported in their quarterly reports.

Let's look at how growth can be supported by the finance department. If the strategy is to grow business by winning new clients, you need to invest in sales and marketing. The more activity an LSP does in this area, the better their chances will be of winning new clients. Obviously, right?

The next step, though, is that once those new clients are won, they will require investment to continue to grow. For each new client, an LSP will need to hire new team members, recruit and train their supply chain, develop quality management programs, and invest in CAT tools. This may not be a profitable venture from day one. There may be several months of expenses before work ramps up and invoices are sent. Then, it might be several more months before the clients pay those invoices. An LSP could very well do six months of work for a new client before they ever see a single dime.

This investment requires cash on hand, and that means it is not enough for the LSP to be growing revenue, but it must also make a profit as this profit can be turned around to invest back into growth. It is the responsibility of the finance department to monitor the business and make sure that the company is growing in a profitable way, with a keen eye for margins. Finance and accounting practices vary from company to company, but typically this means watching three key figures:

- Gross profit: Calculated by deducting the cost of goods sold (COGS) from total revenue. This can be a useful number to watch to make sure that operational tasks are being carried out with efficiency.

- Net profit: Calculated by deducting all other operating expenses, such as general administration costs, costs associated with sales and marketing, and other overhead costs from gross profit.

- EBIDTA: Stands for Earnings Before Interest, Depreciation, Taxes, and Amortization. This is useful particularly for public companies or companies that would like to attract outside investment, as it is a useful tool for external analysts to evaluate a company's performance.

These figures can be calculated for any company by reviewing their financial statements, which are typically prepared every quarter. The finance department prepares and closely monitors these financial statements to make sure that the LSP is healthy, even during periods of growth. LSPs that do not manage their finances properly are easy to recognize over time. Such LSPs are characterized by periods of healthy growth, followed by a period of stagnation. They just cannot keep up with the growth and so they either stop growing or start losing clients because they were not prepared to invest the necessary resources into maintaining healthy growth.

Facilities

Anybody with an internet connection can quickly do a survey of the "Locations" section of different LSPs' websites and see for themselves where most LSPs are concentrated.

If you work at an LSB and have ever had to sit through a PowerPoint sales pitch from an LSP, you have also undoubtedly seen some versions of the "Global Presence" slide. This is the slide where they pull up a world map and put colorful little dots around the globe to mark all of their different locations. Some companies will even show different colored dots to note whether each location is a production hub, a regional sales office, language support hub, or corporate office.

LSPs typically open offices either to be in proximity to their clients or to their vendors. For example, a mature MLSP will have at least three offices worldwide. Offices in Europe, Middle East, and Africa (EMEA), Asia Pacific (APAC), and the Americas will ensure they have 24-hour time zone coverage and therefore can coordinate closely with their suppliers all over the globe. Depending on which customers they are targeting and where those customers are located, one of those offices will also be close to their customer base.

Opening these global offices can get complicated, dealing with local regulations and requiring lots of travel. Therefore, it is a strategy that many MLSPs pursue very cautiously. While expensive, though, it is a necessary step to grow your global manpower and support the Core Functions of project management, vendor management, and sales to allow them to add value for your end clients.

Client Proximity

LSPs looking to engage with tech companies, of course, flock to Seattle and San Francisco. But there are also a large number of LSPs in the Boston area catering to life sciences clients, in Los Angeles to entertainment clients, in Texas to oil and gas clients, and in Montreal to gaming clients. It may cost four times as much to maintain an office in Seattle as it does in Bangalore, but this is a price LSPs are usually willing to pay to be close to their clients. Being in proximity to customers enables the sales team to add value by building a stronger connection with them.

So why do language services providers need to be in close proximity to their clients, if the services they are offering are global? In theory, location shouldn't matter, right? It is because this is what the vast majority of clients need (or at least what they think they need). Even with all the fancy newfangled Skypes and Google Hangouts, at the end of the day, the client wants to have a connection with their language services provider. This connection is hard to make when they are sitting 3,000 miles away or in a completely different time zone. While the idea of the global workforce is very much alive in today's business, it seems that the practice is still lagging behind, as people cling to their old way of doing things.

Vendor Proximity

The second reason LSPs open offices is to be closer to their vendor. But the proximity being referred to here is only related to time zones. It wouldn't be feasible for an LSP to open offices in every single country that they translate for. Fortunately, the vendor relationship is usually much lower maintenance than the client relationship.

Having offices in different time zones means that the production teams can add much more value through the project management Core Function by having full access to the translation vendors during their working hours. Vendor managers also have better access to the linguistic teams and so can better manage the overall relationship with the supply chain. If an LSP's facilities are properly set up, they can have full 24-hour coverage with teams in Asia, Europe and America each working eight-hour days. This means they can add more value to the client without having to work outside of their regular business hours.

Human Resources

Human resources is one of the most overlooked departments in any company, and it is no different in the language services industry. However, it is dangerous for an LSP to not take HR very seriously because on top of the regular HR challenges faced in all industries, there is a whole level of complexity added in a global environment.

For small, local LSPs, it may not be so complicated. If your company is employing a small number of employees in a single location, chances are you may not even have an HR department. Most likely, the human resources functions are being handled by the owner of the company or another manager as just a part of their many duties. However, as a company grows, it is more and more important to start taking a close look at your HR practices to make sure you are set up to succeed.

Labor Laws

Companies that are already global in nature know full well the complexity that comes from managing teams in multiple countries. Each country has different labor laws and practices that need to be taken into account. For those who have been in the language

services industry for any length of time, this has perhaps become common sense, but for people not experienced in international employment, it may not be so intuitive.

Sadly, labor disputes and lawsuits are not an infrequent occurrence in the language services industry. Even the largest, most global LSPs struggle to stay compliant with ever-changing international labor laws, and this can often lead to costly mistakes. Below we discuss the usefulness of opening local offices and supporting them with local human resources departments and the advantages of using professional employer organizations (PEOs) to employ local talent. Both are useful ways of making sure you stay compliant with labor laws. PEOs will be a smart strategy to follow when just starting out in a new country, but as your business and your team grows, it may be prudent to invest in officially expanding your operations to include that country.

Professional Employment Organizations (PEOs)

Many countries have strict laws about who is allowed to employ people, meaning that foreign companies are sometimes not allowed to hire locally. To get around this, LSPs can utilize the services of a PEO to serve as a local intermediary.

Technology

In the good old days, translation was a very manual process. Documents were mailed to translators, who would translate the content (on typewriters) and mail it back. There was no email. There were no CAT tools. Just to put it in perspective: One of Renato's first business expenses when he started his first translation company was a fax machine, which he bought for US $1,500. Those were the days!

> **Tools Commonly Used by LSPs**
> **TMS** — Translation management system
> **QMS** — Query management system
> **TM** — Translation memory
> **CAT** — Computer-aided translation
> **MT** — Machine translation
> **AutoLQA** — Automated language quality assurance
> **SCMS** — Supply chain management systems

Today, times have changed, of course, and they continue to change. Technology has become integral to the language services industry, whether we like it or not. Translation management systems (TMSs) help LSBs and LSPs manage complex content libraries; integrated computer-aided translation (CAT) and translation memories (TM) drastically reduce word count; and query management systems (QMS) and automated language quality assurance (AutoLQA) systems improve quality by giving translators the tools they need to more efficiently perform their work. MT is improving every day and is helping cost-sensitive LSBs translate volumes of content that were previously unthinkable.

What all these technologies have in common is that they increase efficiency. Increased efficiency leads to higher throughput for lower cost. It is no small wonder that technology is the number one topic discussed in the language services industry.

We already discussed technology and automation in the context of the Market Influencer evaluation. We looked at technology specifically when discussing substitute services such as MT and process automation. But if you were paying attention you will notice that technology and automation is a theme that runs through all of the five Market Influencers, more than any other factor we have discussed so far. Technology is the driving force behind the evolution of the language services industry. LSPs are being asked to do more with less, and until we perfect our translator cloning process, the only way to do this is through technology and automation.

Technology supports the vendor management Core Function by providing systems for tracking increasingly complex supply chains. In years past, supply chains were built out of the Yellow Pages and managed out of a Rolodex. Binders full of business cards represented your trusted suppliers. Today, complex databases can be built to track supplier

information, including availability, rates, specialization, and any other data that you would like to include. Many TMSs also come preloaded with supply chain (vendor) management systems.

Project managers enjoy perhaps the most benefit from technology, as they can use TMSs and CAT tools to help manage the translation process. These tools are becoming increasingly integrated. Each new update rolls out new features that assist the project manager, even going so far as to completely automate many aspects of the project management Core Function. As we have mentioned previously, full process automation is the Holy Grail of the language services industry and so a lot of investment has gone into this area. Technology has not yet fully replaced the need for project management, but it is developing quickly. Taking advantage of the technology that is available today, a single project manager can efficiently handle the work that would have taken 10 project managers as recently as a decade ago.

Even salespersons can benefit from new technologies. Customer relationship management systems (CRMs) are not unique to the industry, but they are nonetheless very useful tools for helping LSPs carry out the value-add activities of sales. Such technology allows salespersons to better understand the specific needs of each customer and provide them with specialized consulting and match them with the language services that meet their needs.

Technology is, and will continue to be, the most influential driving force behind the ongoing evolution of the language services industry. We feel fully confident putting this statement in print because this basic truth will not change in the near future. It doesn't matter if you are reading this book hot off the presses or found it in a Barnes & Noble clearance bin 10 years hence. The need for increased efficiencies is not going anywhere. LSBs will continue to demand more for less and LSPs will continue to turn to the newest technologies and automations to meet this demand.

Language Quality Assurance

Finally, we get to the topic of quality. You may have noticed that we have not talked about quality so much in this book. You may have also noticed that quality assurance is classified as a Support Activity rather than a Core Function. How is it that sales  is a Core Function and quality is only a Support Activity, you may be ask. Has there been some sort of mistake? The answer is simple. Quality assurance is not a Core Function of the LSP because it does not add value.

Let us explain using an example that most of us can relate to. Have you ever hired a plumber? (If you haven't, then, just say yes and pretend for a while, it will make this go quicker.) Being a savvy consumer, you probably did some research to look up multiple plumbers and compare their quality by reading online reviews. Most likely, any plumber with even a single negative review was immediately removed from your selection process. You are then left with a list of five plumbers who have good ratings. You then picked the one that was the least expensive (price sensitivity), or perhaps the one that was closest to you (availability), or maybe the one that was referred to you by a friend (a form of customer loyalty). Now, if you hire that plumber and he does a good job for you, you may hire him for the next job or you may not. But if he does a bad job, you will most certainly never work with him again.

Quality was the first thing that you looked for in your search, but it is not the reason you hired. This is because quality is a requirement, not a perk. Plumbers don't get paid to do a good job, they get paid to do a job, and the expectation is that it is good.

Language services is no different. LSPs are expected to deliver good quality translations. They don't get extra credit for it. One of the biggest and most common mistakes made by LSPs is that they think they can differentiate themselves on quality. Every LSP brags about their quality, claiming that it is better than their competitors. However, all of their competitors are claiming that they have the best quality. The reality is that quality is indistinguishable from company to company.

This is not to downplay the importance of language quality, though. To the contrary, strong quality management practices are crucial for an LSP. Without it, you will be fired, just like you would fire a plumber that messed up your toilet installation. What we are saying is that low quality will most certainly lose customers, but high quality is not necessarily enough to keep them.

BAD QUALITY IS ENOUGH TO LOSE A CUSTOMER, BUT GOOD QUALITY ISN'T ENOUGH TO KEEP THEM.

Remember that LSBs do not usually understand the languages they are requesting. To them, language is a deliverable that either meets expectations or it doesn't. Most of the time they will not even be able to recognize quality when they see it. When an LSB purchases services from the industry, they are not buying quality. They are buying the value that is added through the language services value chain.

Good LQA practices enable an LSP to continue adding value through the Core Functions. LQA processes ensure that your supply chain is well qualified and competent through the vendor management Core Function. Project managers need to rely upon the LQA process so that they can deliver high quality services to the customer. Fewer quality issues mean less time spent on project management to fix mistakes and less time spent through the sales Function to manage unhappy customers.

The Three Core Functions

Referring to our diagram of the General Theory of the Translation Company, we see that the LSP is surrounded by Market Influencers and supported by Support Activities. The Core Functions performed by the LSP are at the center of the diagram. The main difference between the Support Activities and the Core functions in the middle is very simple. Both are necessary activities that need to be carried out by the LSP, but the Core Functions in the middle represent the LSP's core competencies that add value to the language services value chain. It is through these Core Functions that the LSP is going to develop a meaningful differentiation between themselves and their clients.

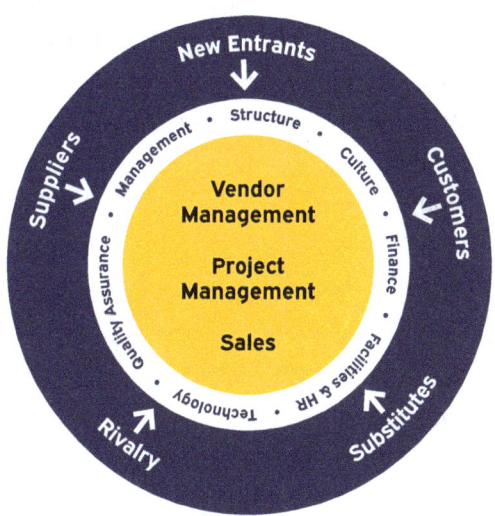

Figure 16: Core Functions and the values they enable.

This is not to downplay the importance of the Market Influencer evaluation or Support Activities. Without the former, you will not know the challenges and opportunities and you will struggle to find your niche in the industry. Without the latter, you will not be able to effectively deliver on your Core Functions.

This book intentionally focuses on the Core Functions last, even though they are certainly the most exciting to talk about. We could have written an entire book just about these. However, while it is tempting to focus only on Core Functions, this would be a backwards way of approaching the industry. Rather than thinking of the Core Functions as being more important than the Market Influencer evaluation or Support Activities, it would be more useful to think of the Core Competencies as the result of them.

We hope that one of the key takeaways from this book will be for our LSP readers who will walk away feeling more empowered to attain success. As we have already seen, this is a complex and ever-changing industry and it is tempting to fall into despair and focus on factors that you don't have any control over. This is the chapter where we focus on the areas on which you will absolutely be able to exert the most amount of influence. The decisions and strategies executed through these Core Functions will be informed by your strategic market analysis and enabled by your Support Activities. In our previous discussions we have set ourselves up with the knowledge and infrastructure to be able to execute in the three key areas of vendor management, project management, and sales. These directly lead you to meaningful ways of differentiating yourself from the competition by adding value to your clients.

Note that we are using the terminology 'Core Functions', rather than the more commonly used 'core competencies'. This is quite intentional and represents an important distinction. We

CORE FUNCTIONS ARE THE KEY ACTIVITIES OF AN LSP THAT DIRECTLY ADD VALUE TO THE LANGUAGE SERVICES VALUE CHAIN.

believe that the term 'competencies' can too easily be assigned to individuals or groups of individuals within a company. We use the term 'functions' because it is very important to remember that these are functions that can be carried out by anybody in an LSP.

When we discuss the project management Core Function, for example, it doesn't necessarily mean that it is entirely carried out by a project manager. The functions of project management could be split between multiple people, regardless of their titles. Conversely, in a small company, it is entirely possible that one person such as the owner carries out aspects of all three Core Functions by himself. In both of these examples, the titles are not as important as the functions that are carried out. This is why we use the terminology 'Core Functions'. If you prefer, though, you are free to use the terms 'Functions' and 'Competencies' interchangeably, so long as you keep in mind that we are talking about functions that are carried out and not the individuals or groups doing them.

Language Services Buyers (LSBs)			
Massive Multiple Language Service Provider (MMLSP)	OR	Multiple Language Service Provider (MLSP)	
Regional Multiple Language Services Provider (RMLSP) EMEA	Regional Multiple Language Services Provider (RMLSP) APAC		Regional Multiple Language Services Provider (RMLSP) Americas
Local In-Country Single-Language Service Provider (SLSP)	Local In-Country Single-Language Service Provider (SLSP)	Local In-Country Single-Language Service Provider (SLSP)	Local In-Country Single-Language Service Provider (SLSP)
Contracted Language Professional (CLP)	Contracted Language Professional (CLP)	Contracted Language Professional (CLP)	Contracted Language Professional (CLP)	Contracted Language Professional (CLP)

We looked at the key players in the language services value chain back in the very first section of this book. It is comprised of the many different layers of LSPs and CLPs that work together to add value to the end customer: the LSB.

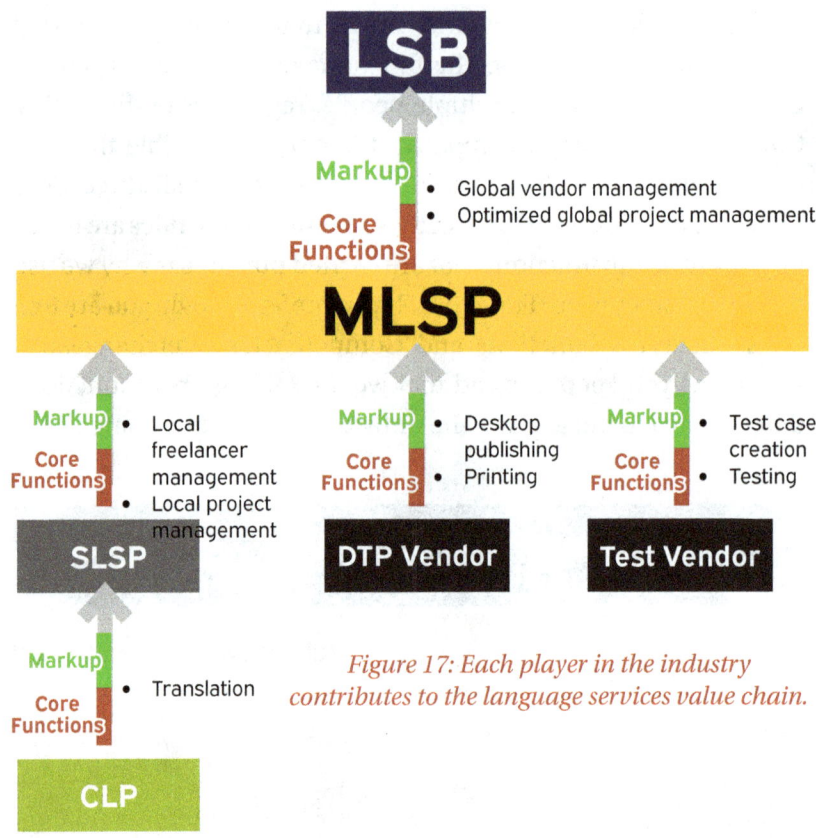

Figure 17: Each player in the industry contributes to the language services value chain.

Looking again at the value chain, we recognize that there is a whole lot of outsourcing going on, particularly when it comes to the 'language' part of language services. There seems to be a very long distance between the actual buyers of language services at the top and the translators (CLPs) at the bottom. Why are there so many steps, so many different companies between the buyer and the producers? We hope that by the end of this book, the answer to this question becomes abundantly clear. Each player in the language services value chain provides value-add services through their Core Function and marks up their services appropriately to add more value to the process. As the work flows up from the bottom of the value chain, the amount of accumulated value has increased, which justifies the higher price to the language services buyers.

The end result is that the final product (or service) provided to the LSB is of much higher value than if they were to purchase directly from the translators. Any activities that are not Core Functions do not directly create value, but rather indirectly create value by supporting the Core Functions. The freelance translator creates value through translation, since that is their Core Function. The LSP creates value through vendor management, project management, and sales. Each step in the process adds additional value.

This section further explores each of the three Core Functions and demonstrates how they add value to the language services value chain.

The Vendor Management Core Function

Some years ago, Renato was put in charge of the vendor management team for a global MMLSP. The company had been going through some major transitions at the time and there was a lot of confusion around their vendor strategy. There were no clear expectations from the vendor management team and this lack of clarity extended into the team itself. Over the previous five years, they had been through so many changes as a team, nobody was even sure any more what their job was or how to do it. Recognizing the lack of clarity in his team, Renato pulled everybody into the same room and asked them one question: "What is your job?"

There were plenty of answers from the team members. "Decrease supply chain costs!" one person responded. Another answered, "Manage vendor relationships!" A third person shouted, "Improve vendor quality!" There seemed to be as many different answers as there were people in the room and none of the answers were necessarily incorrect.

"Let's slow down," Renato said. "We are overcomplicating this." At the basest level, what is our job as vendor managers? Give me an answer in two words." The team thought about this. In a way, this was an insulting question, as it was asking them to distill their very challenging job down into two words, which could not possibly capture the complexities of their work. Renato answered: "Find people."

The job of the vendor management team is to find people. Now of course, there are a lot of other activities that need to happen for the vendor manager to find people, but at the core of it, the mandate is very simple. Find people.

LSPs rarely employ in-house linguists. Most linguistic services are outsourced, either to smaller LSPs or to freelance CLPs. Without these suppliers, LSP cannot do the basic function it is expected to do, which is of course to provide language services. This is why vendor management is such a crucial function for the LSP. The vendor manager must define and carry out a structured program for recruiting and managing talent that will be performing the services for the client.

This chapter explores in greater detail how the vendor management carries out this basic mandate. It is important, though, for us to remind you once again, that as we are discussing this, or any of the Core Functions of the LSP, we are discussing functions, not the people.

> THE JOB OF A VENDOR MANAGER IS TO FIND PEOPLE.

We use the term vendor management to describe this function, but it doesn't matter if it is called supply chain management, procurement, talent acquisition, or anything else. The function is the same. Sometimes, vendor management responsibilities are even carried out by the project manager or the engineer. Sometimes in small companies, the owner is doing everything herself. So keep in mind while we are discussing these concepts that, even if your job title is not supply chain manager, it is likely that you may find some of the ideas discussed below are relevant to your function within the organization.

Creating Value

As we have stated, defined in two words or less, the vendor manager's job is to find people. One could argue that it is a vendor manager's job to find good people. We wouldn't disagree with you. We would simply point out that is three words and it should be understood that of course we want to find good people. Vendor managers need to find good people who add value. Good people add value, value ads money, money increases margin. Simple as that.

One of the worst mistakes that a vendor manager could make is to focus only on price. This happens all the time. Of course, it is necessary to consider price of the vendor before making a selection. Of course, a vendor manager needs to negotiate the best possible price with the selected vendors. Of course, some projects will have a very tight budget, so price will be an important decision-making factor. However, price is only one consideration that needs to be evaluated before selecting which external vendors to engage with.

Each time a vendor manager selects a vendor to work with, there needs to be a cost/benefit analysis, where you weigh the costs and risks associated with a vendor against the potential benefits of working with that vendor. But notice here that we have drawn a subtle distinction between price and cost. Cost is not only price, but also includes the total cost of doing business with a certain vendor, whereas price is only a number on a purchase order.

While inexperienced vendor managers focus on price, more mature ones will also look at a list of other factors that have the potential to add/decrease value, such as timeliness, responsiveness, quality of work, customer service, breadth of experience, flexibility, availability, proactivity, scalability, location, openness to teamwork, and the list could go on and on. How well a vendor ranks in any of these categories will affect how much value they are adding to the process. Each of these factors needs to be considered to calculate the best value of each vendor according to the project requirements. The best value represents the net value that is added to an individual engagement from different factors that are weighted according to the requirements of the engagement and considering the sum of the actual and potential costs.

Every project is different, so there is no set process for calculating best value for all engagements. Different factors are weighted differently for each project. Let's say that you have a very quick project that needs to be delivered as soon as possible to your client. In such a scenario, you would necessarily place more importance on speed than on quality. For another project, you have a comfortable timeline, but the client is very sensitive to quality. So, you would not place as much value on speed for this project because if you rush it, the quality may be unacceptable. In situations like these, it is up to the vendor manager to weigh each factor based on importance to find the best value.

THE BEST VALUE REPRESENTS THE NET VALUE THAT IS ADDED TO AN ENGAGEMENT FROM DIFFERENT FACTORS THAT ARE WEIGHTED ACCORDING TO THE REQUIREMENTS OF THE ENGAGEMENT AND CONSIDERING THE SUM OF THE ACTUAL AND POTENTIAL COSTS.

To do this, the vendor manager will need to perform two evaluations. The first evaluation is to understand the requirements of the project. The second evaluation is to understand the net value of a vendor, broken down into different value categories. Once these evaluations are complete, you can tie them together to compare vendors and select the one with the best value for that project.

Project Requirement Evaluation

The first step is to understand the requirements for the project or program you are looking to find a vendor for. This could be a single project, or it could be a large ongoing program. The only requirement is that the project or program should have consistent requirements. For example, if you are evaluating the requirements for an ongoing program, then those requirements should not change from project to project within that program. Every project in that program, for example, should have similar requirements for quality, timeliness, etc. Once you have defined the scope of the program you would like to evaluate, you need to list the requirements for any vendor that would be working on that program. Price will be a requirement for virtually any program, so that will most likely be at the top of your list. For example, you would start with a list that looks something like this:

Requirements
Price
Timeliness
Quality
Location
Scalability
Experience

Once you have your list of requirements, add a column to rank how important each of those requirements is on a scale of 1 to 10. We call this the specific value multiplier (SVM). It should go without saying that not all requirements should be 10. If you are tempted to list everything as a 10, then you need to learn how to prioritize better, which unfortunately is not a lesson that we intend to teach in this book. For example, a small rush project may have an SVM of 10 for timeliness, but only 5 for quality, as in this example below:

Requirements	Specific Value Multiplier (0-10)
Price	5
Timeliness	10
Quality	5
Location	1
Scalability	8
Experience	6

With the SVM determined for each factor, there is now a clear picture of how important different requirements are for your project. These will be the criteria that are used to evaluate different vendors to calculate their best value for this project.

Vendor Evaluation

It is important to rank vendors according to the same scale in order for the calculations to work properly and you should rank them in the same areas identified in the project requirement evaluation.

Vendor #1

Requirements	Vendor Ranking (1-10)
Price	8
Timeliness	1
Quality	0
Location	5
Scalability	5
Experience	5
Total:	24

Vendor #2

Requirements	Vendor Ranking (1-10)
Price	2
Timeliness	8
Quality	6
Location	1
Scalability	1
Experience	2
Total:	20

You will notice in the above example we have totaled the value of each vendor according to the ranking for each category. Vendor #1 has a value of 24 points, whereas vendor #2 only has a value of 20 points. At first glance, this would lead us to conclude that we should work with Vendor #1, as it is the higher value vendor. But not so fast....

Selecting the Right Vendor

Remember that our goal is to find the best value for each vendor, which means their value needs to be evaluated in the context of the project requirements. So our next step is to combine our two evaluations together to get the best value evaluation. This is done by multiplying the specific value for each category in the vendor evaluation by the value multiplier in the project requirements evaluation to get the weighted value for each category. The sum of these weighted values gives us the best value for this engagement.

Vendor #1

Requirements	Value Multiplier (1-10)	Vendor Ranking (1-10)	Weighted
Price	5	8	40
Timeliness	10	1	10
Quality	5	0	0
Location	1	5	5
Scalability	8	5	40
Experience	6	5	30
Total:	35	24	125

Vendor #2

Requirements	Value Multiplier (1-10)	Vendor Ranking (1-10)	Weighted
Price	5	8	10
Timeliness	10	2	80
Quality	5	6	30
Location	1	1	1
Scalability	8	1	8
Experience	6	2	12
Total:	35	20	141

As we can see from the example on page 142, it turns out that vendor #2 actually has a higher value than vendor #1, even though at first glance vendor #1 seemed like it was adding more value. This illustrates nicely the importance of looking at best value in the context of each individual vendor engagement.

Improvised vs. Structured Vendor Management

We have described the vendor management Core Function as being responsible for adding value to the LSP's service offerings by defining and carrying out a structured program for recruiting and managing talent that will be performing the services being sold to the client. We've made an important distinction in this definition, which is that the vendor manager is able to add value by having a structured program.

This leads us to a discussion on the difference between improvised and structured vendor management. The goal of the vendor management function is to have as much structure around their program as possible while still being able to respond to the needs of the clients. When we say "as structured as possible," we are not setting the bar low out of laziness, either. We are being realists.

Improvised

- "Oh shit—we need to find people because we just signed a contract!"
- "We will hire the first people to respond to the job posting, even if they are expensive!"
- "Whatever it takes to get the job done, even if we have to cut corners—let's do this!"

Structured

- "Let's check our database to see which vendors have the best value for this new client."
- "The sales pipeline is pretty full, we better prepare by onboarding new vendors."
- "We need to carefully vet each new vendor."

To survive in the language services industry, a high degree of flexibility and improvisation is needed. Not everything can be structured into a nice codified process. Indeed, not everything should always be completely structured, as that could lead to loss of organizational agility. Companies that add too much structure around their vendor management process will inevitably find that they have created a system in which they are not able to respond to the ever-changing needs of their customers. There needs to be balance.

Improvised Vendor Management

Improvised (or flexible) vendor management is the baseline. This is where most new companies start out. We could call it reactive vendor management, but have chosen not to because we find that the term "reactive" is highly loaded and often carries a negative connotation. Strictly speaking, improvised vendor management is, indeed, very reactive, but it is necessarily so.

There are certainly downsides to following an improvised strategy. When we performed our Market Influencer evaluation, we saw how bargaining power of suppliers and purchasers can work for or against the LSP to drive prices up or down. By taking a reactionary approach to vendor management, an LSP is essentially shifting more of this bargaining power into the hands of their supply chain. In a structured vendor management model, an LSP proactively builds a network of CLPs and SLSPs prepared to accept work. Multiple vendors can be onboarded so as to decrease their collective bargaining power and drive down their prices. Well-defined contracts and service level agreements (SLAs) can be put into place and volume discounts can be negotiated. These things all take time and so none of these things are possible with an improvised program.

There is no such thing as "improvised strategy". With improvised vendor management, an LSP is constantly in crisis mode, jumping from one sourcing request to the next. There is little time to negotiate price or perform best value evaluations. What this means is that vendors will get selected because they were available and willing to accept the job or because they are the cheapest. Neither of these scenarios leaves room for a close examination of the vendor. This effectively diminishes the amount of value that the vendor manager is able to contribute to the client. Rather than being a value adding step in the process, the vendor manager function is reduced to simple crisis management.

For example, a small MLSP that is just starting out may not have the resources needed to invest into a mature vendor management program and so must fall back on improvisation. Perhaps they have made a business decision to de-prioritize investment into vendor management and focus instead on areas more directly related to growing their business, such as sales and project management. This is a common case among smaller LSPs, who do not have access to the money and resources needed to roll out more advanced processes.

Let's say that this small MLSP wins a new contract for translating a pharmaceutical patent from German to Polish. Chances are they don't have a whole team of German to Polish translators specialized in life sciences contract translations that they can call up. So, they will have to improvise. They are forced to pursue a very reactionary way of approaching vendor management since the strategy is driven completely by the client's needs. In the absence of structure, an improvised vendor management strategy is better than no vendor strategy. At that time, it was an absolutely necessity to improvise.

However, what would happen if they were approaching this in a more strategic way? It would mean that the MLSP would have been proactively collecting and maintaining information on potential resources that could work on such projects. As soon as the contract with the customer was signed, there would already be some translators in the database, one of whom would be selected based on the results of the best value analysis.

However, pursuing such a structured strategy would mean that the vendor management team would be tasked with sourcing talent for virtually any possible scenario to prepare for the likelihood of receiving a project. Ain't nobody got time for that. It's just not feasible, no matter how large the MLSP or how much they want to invest in a structured vendor management strategy. The point is that regardless how large an MLSP is or how structured vendor management strategy is, there will still be times when it is absolutely critical to be flexible and to react quickly to meet the customer's needs. Structure is better than no structure, but there will always be "last resort" situations that call for improvisation.

Structured Vendor Management Strategy

When we made the point in the previous example that improvised vendor management was necessary for the given situation, note that we made the important qualifier: "at that time". So when we say it is necessary, we mean it in the way that an emergency back alley appendectomy performed with a rusty spork is necessary if there is no better option. Basically, it was necessary to improvise then because there was no better strategy that could be followed to meet the customer's needs. Immediate and swift action was needed. The goal of structured vendor management is to put systems and processes in place that are able to reduce the number of situations where improvised reaction is needed.

While improvised vendor management is about action, structured vendor management is about strategy and planning. Structured vendor management is like a grandmaster playing a game of chess, always thinking 10 moves ahead. Improvised vendor management is like Tucker playing chess—reacting frantically to each move, lots of sweating and cursing involved, and trying to cheat while his opponent is in the bathroom.

Structured vendor management anticipates the demand the LSP will have on the supply chain and proactively takes steps to meet these needs. For a company that specializes in certain languages or verticals, this can be a relatively simple process. Does your LSP work mostly on legal translations into European languages? Then great, you can proactively build a supply chain specialized in this area for major European languages, so that you are not caught off guard if a very large new project comes in. You can even build extra capacity to manage the spikes in volume that may come. You can perform an evaluation for each of the vendors that you onboard and store these in an organized database, ready to be pulled up for an analysis for each new project that comes through the door.

Thinking ahead, you can proactively negotiate reduced rates with vendors because you may be in a position to provide them much more work than they would otherwise get. Rather than negotiating price on a project-by-project basis, you are able to negotiate price on a program basis. This is often seen in the form of a volume discount, where vendors are willing and happy to lower their rates if an LSP can guarantee them a certain amount of work. For a large MLSP, there may be a dozen project managers working on a dozen different customers. Each one of these programs may be somewhat small, so there can be no volume discount for each individual project. This is where the vendor management is able to add value by representing the combined bargaining power of all of those programs to negotiate better terms with the vendors, adding value to each of those different programs.

In the example given to illustrate the need for improvised vendor management, our MLSP received a project that was completely outside of their core competencies. Perhaps they had never translated pharmaceutical contracts before. Perhaps they had never worked on German to Polish translations either. That is why they found themselves in a situation where they needed to be reactionary rather than strategic; to act rather than plan.

Even though this project was completely outside of the company's core business, this situation still could have been mitigated by structuring the way in which vendors are recruited and onboarded. Processes could be rolled out for the vendor manager to have more visibility into the sales pipeline so that upcoming supply chain demands could be properly forecasted and recruitment could start ahead of time. It is rare that a new client signs a contract without any warning. Usually, the sales team talks to a client for weeks or months before a new project is won. By analyzing the opportunities that the sales team is working on, a vendor manager can proactively start aligning resources to meet the needs of the new customers. It is in the sales team's best interest, as well, because it means that their new clients are going to get the maximum benefits out of vendor management.

Strategic Vendor Management

It is useful to think of vendor management in terms of an Emergency Room. If you get rolled into the Emergency Room on a stretcher, the last thing you want is for your doctors and nurses to improvise. This is why there are processes in place in Emergency Rooms to ensure that the care you receive is of the best possible value. There is structure.

However, what happens when there are circumstances that were not planned for? During a natural disaster or after a crazy English soccer riot, there will perhaps not be enough medical professionals on staff. Perhaps there will be a shortage of plasma transfusions. There will not be enough beds or rooms available. In such a case, you will be happy that the medical staff is able to improvise by having nurses fill in for doctors or creating improvised beds in the hallways to accommodate the overflow. Not ideal, of course, but better than the alternative.

Likewise, for localization, there will always be times when

improvisation is needed. It is not ideal, but it is sometimes necessary. Vendor management, just like project management, is hard. It is really hard. But this is good news for the LSP, because if it were easy, the customers would do it themselves. This is an area where LSPs can add a lot of value for their clients and they do so not just by having a structured vendor management strategy in place, but also by improvising. There needs to be room for both.

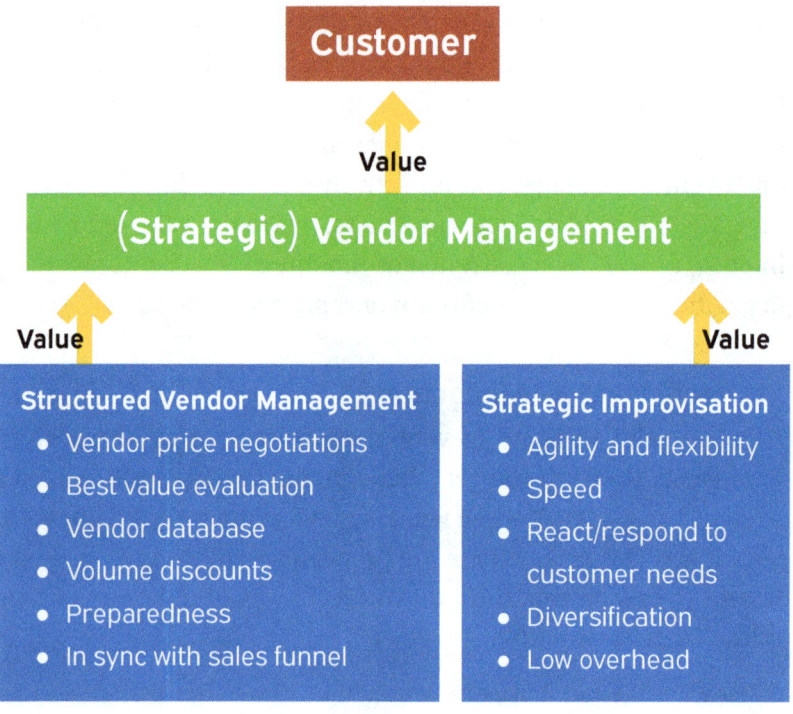

Figure 18: The different ways in which structured as well as improvised vendor management add value.

We have seen small MLSPs fail to scale their supply chain because they are unable to implement structured vendor management processes. We have also seen large MMLSPs struggle because they focused too much on the structure and forgot how to improvise. An MMLSP may be so structured that there is no room for quick action. Often what happens in such an organization is that the vendor managers begin to think of themselves more as relationship managers with their existing supply chains. They have built a supply chain that is able to meet the needs of the MLSP, so they focus their energy on managing the relationship with that supply chain, rather than recruiting new vendors to work on new projects. After a while, the vendor management department grows complacent and loses the skills necessary to recruit new talented and experienced suppliers into the supply chain. They forget their one job as a vendor manager: Find people.

There needs to be room for both structure and action, both planning and improvisation. While it is not ideal to have completely random, reactionary, improvised vendor management, an LSP still needs to hold on to the flexibility. Above, we made the point that there is no such thing as "improvised strategy." However, there is absolutely a thing such as "strategic improvisation."

Strategic improvisation, combined with structured vendor management, puts into place best practices and systems that facilitate a strategic model. Such a system will allow for your vendor management program to be structured as much as possible, but still allow for fast thinking and quick responses that are so often necessary to meet the needs of your customers. Strategic vendor management is a righteous goal for vendor managers, but it is important to not lose sight of the why. Strategic vendor management is simply a tool—a tool that is used to help the vendor manager carry out their primary responsibility, which is to find people.

Freelancers, LSPs, and Best Value

When we say that a vendor manager's job is to find people, this can mean different things. For a small SLP that relies upon a network for freelance CLPs to perform the work, finding people literally means finding people. For a larger MLSP who engages with smaller SLSPs, finding people may mean that you are actually finding companies full of people to do the work, which can be more expensive than working directly with freelance CLPs. Each additional layer that you add to the supply chain increases the price you pay. But remember, there is a big difference between price and cost.

SLSPs typically sell their services to MLSPs. Occasionally, an LSB will contract directly with CLPs that is, the end customer hires freelancers directly in an effort to reduce costs, but most localization programs run through the standard supply chain. The reason most localization programs are set up this way is because most of what is bought and sold in the language services industry is not actually language services, but rather the value added through the Core Functions.

Each player in the language services value chain adds value by purchasing services from downstream providers, performing a set of project management services themselves, and selling the result to their customers upstream. Those who have been around in the industry for any time realize the benefits of this system and work with it. However, there is always talk of shortening the supply chain and therefore reducing costs.

This experiment typically takes the form of either an LSB or an MLSP attempting to work directly with CLPs, effectively cutting out the intermediary LSPs and working directly with the translators. Such an effort always starts with good intentions and, in theory at least, there's no reason why it shouldn't work. The logic is that by working directly with the translators, not only will prices go down, but there will be better communication between the end client and the translators who are performing the work. This increased communication, it is thought, will lead to better translations because the translators are more in touch with the needs of the end customer. Furthermore, the speed of delivery should improve because projects pass through fewer hands on their way to the translator and back to the client. Usually, there is a proposed tool or piece of software that is going to facilitate this entire process and everything will be fully automated. It sounds like the perfect plan. Nothing could go wrong!

If you have attended industry conferences and listened to speakers, you have surely at some point heard somebody talking about revolutionizing the industry by shortening the supply chain. Despite what that fast-talking LSP salesperson told you, this is not a revolutionary concept. In fact, it is quite an old concept. It has been tried many times before. Mostly it has failed. However, there is always a fresh new startup or a self-proclaimed visionary in the industry ready to claim that now they are onto something: this time it is going to work! We've all heard speeches or attended webinars from passionate language services professionals who are claiming that they have a shiny new tool or brand-new process that is going to shorten the supply chain and revolutionize the entire way we do business. The first few times we heard these speeches, we believed them. However, after a decade or two in the industry, you begin to recognize them for what they are: nonsense. Well intentioned and passionate, but nonsense nonetheless.

What these well-intentioned visionaries forget is the entire reason for the standard localization supply chain in the first place. They think that LSPs sell translation. If LSPs actually sold translation, it would make perfect sense to cut out as many intermediaries as possible. But LSPs do not sell translation, they sell

project management. When you cut players out of the supply chain, you are also cutting valuable services. Without the SLSP to manage the freelancers or the MLSP to manage the many different languages, the burden is now on the LSB to manage everything themselves, which is a feat that few LSBs are prepared for. Any cost savings are quickly negated by increased project management effort for all the time spent performing the tasks that would typically be performed by the intermediary LSPs.

The Project Management Core Function

It is not by accident that the project management Core Function is at the center of everything. This is where it all comes together. The project management function is the single most important part of the entire language services provider. This is a fundamental truth, so we will repeat ourselves. The project management function is the single most important part of the entire language services provider. We realize this may be a somewhat controversial statement, so please allow us to explain ourselves in the following section.

Project management, at its basic level, can be designed as the process of managing resources within the constraints of the Market Influencers and Support Activities to add value to the customer. Resources can be defined as people, time, technology, and money, basically everything a company uses to deliver to their client. Sometimes this can mean that the project manager function is even responsible for managing the other two Core Functions of vendor management and sales!

Where we often misunderstand the importance of project management is that we think it is only carried out by project managers. Project management is a function, not a title. Undoubtedly, many readers who cringed at our assertion that project management is the single most important function for an LSP

may be forgetting this, thinking that we meant to imply that project managers are the most important people. So, for the purposes of this section, please keep in mind that even if we are using examples with project managers, these could easily be replaced by other team members who carry out the same functions.

In the diagram below we have identified project management as the function of managing resources in order to add value to the client. The project manager, working within the constraints of the market influencers and LSP infrastructure, is responsible for aligning the resources of people, time, technology, and money in order to create value for the end client.

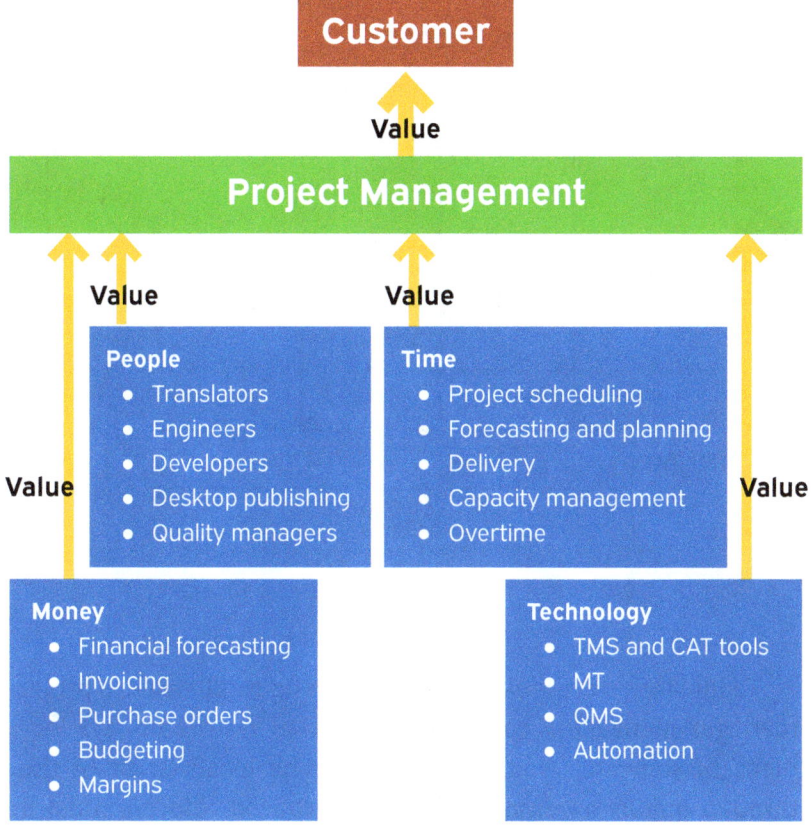

Figure 19: Project management is the function of managing resources in order to add value to the client.

People

Not all project managers actually have people reporting into them, though it is not uncommon that they have their own teams. But when we talk about project managers managing people, we need to broaden the conversation to include everyone being coordinated by the project manager and not just the team that reports to the project manager. For example, a project manager may coordinate resources in an LSP across multiple geographic offices. Those team members may be reporting to regional managers for each location officially, but for the purposes of the projects, they are essentially reporting to the project manager.

Website Localization Process

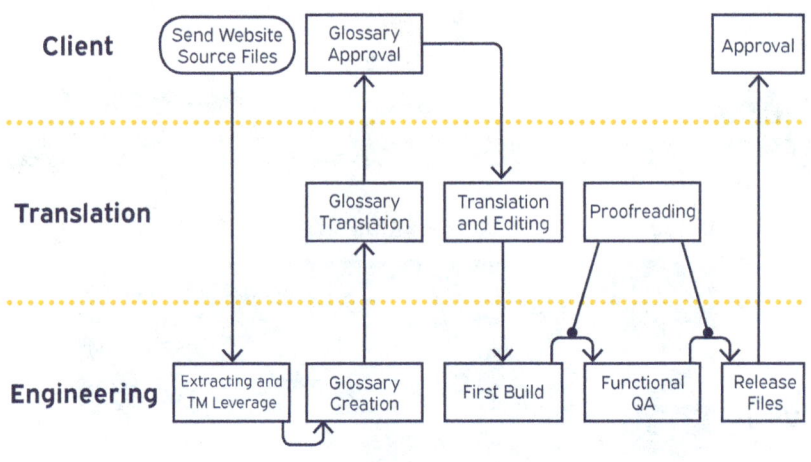

Figure 20: A workflow for website localization.

To illustrate, let's look at a situation in figure 20 where a project manager manages a complex localization testing project for a piece of software. First, the files must be localized, then they through quality assurance. The final localized software must be tested by language testers to make sure there are no bugs or issues. The project manager, of course, is responsible for overseeing the entire process. The process workflow would look roughly as shown in the example. Note: for those of you cringing at the simplicity of the workflow, keep in mind that this is for illustrative purposes only, and that actual workflows may be much more complex in reality.

The engineering team may report to a completely different manager, officially. Perhaps the project manager will have to coordinate with a separate shared services team for help with the glossary creation. For the final functional QA step, there may be yet another team in China reporting to a regional manager. Regardless of the official reporting structure though, the project manager is the one responsible for coordinating and managing all the different people in the workflow to ensure that the project is completed successfully. The fact that these other team members do not report directly to the project manager limits his control over this process and adds an additional layer of complexity to the project management process.

The organizational structure is based on how you defined your teams to better compete in your niche. This is so important that we dedicated a whole section to it when we talked about the Seven Support Activities of an LSP. As you are probably beginning to realize, the ability of an LSP to carry out the project management Core Function is directly affected by how it is structured. Let's discuss some of the challenges faced by project managers when dealing with different organizational structures.

Direct Reports

Sometimes it makes sense to have teams reporting directly to project managers. Some of the people that could commonly report to a project manager would be junior project managers, localization engineers or quality managers. Additionally, technology managers, desktop publishing experts, testing managers, and other roles could also report directly to the project manager, but frequently don't. The organizational setup of a team can and does look very different from company to company and even from project to project.

An advantage to having direct reports to the project manager is that it gives her a higher level of control over the team members. As a people manager, the project manager literally controls their time and can easily and quickly manage how the team members are allocating their time and where. Flexibility and agility are needed when managing complex localization projects and it is useful for a project manager to be able to quickly reallocate team members where they are needed. If the project team members are not reporting directly to the project manager, then she needs to negotiate with their direct manager in order to allocate the time needed.

In an LSP where there are multiple clients, all with multiple projects and competing deadlines, it can become difficult to know how to prioritize each task. Everybody is busy all the time so every time a task is worked on, it means there is another lower priority task that is not being worked on. If the project manager is managing the localization engineers directly, she has full control over how they are prioritizing their time. She has the authority to prioritize their time to make sure that this task is performed efficiently, also while balancing the needs of other projects that are no doubt happening simultaneously. For example, if an important client has a very high priority project, the project manager can have the localization engineer drop whatever they are doing and get this done as soon as possible. This is as simple as an email or a phone call to the localization engineer to make sure that they understand the importance and to get to work immediately.

However, there are also disadvantages to project managers directly managing their teams. Sometimes they are working on teams spread out globally and it may make more sense to have the global team members report to local managers. In localization, it is very rare for any team to have the luxury of everyone sitting in the same office. The project manager's challenge becomes bigger if she is responsible for the direct management of those team members. On top of managing every aspect of the process, she will now have to become a true personnel manager and take on all of the responsibilities associated with this role, which can be very time-consuming.

All too often, we see project managers failing because they are given direct reports but are not properly trained on how to manage people. They may be great process managers, but managing people is a whole different ball of wax. If the project managers are to succeed in this area, they will need to work closely with their team members to set quarterly/yearly goals, hold weekly one-on-one meetings with each direct report, deal with underperforming team members, do salary reviews, and motivate their team. Being a people manager means playing many roles: teacher, counselor, hostage negotiator, HR lawyer, recruiter, and occasional executioner. This is a lot of responsibility for anybody. For project managers it means that they will be left with much less time for more value-add tasks as their time will be spent on Support Activities, which they are oftentimes not well-equipped to do.

So while there are certainly benefits to organizing teams with solid accountability to project management, there are also costs associated with such a strategy. Fortunately, the project management function can be carried out without having to load the project manager with extra Support Activity responsibilities. Teams can be organized separately and asked to collaborate under the guidance of the project manager.

Indirect Reports

When most people think about the setup of a localization program, they may think of a hierarchical structure set up with various functions reporting to the Project Manager who oversees the entire process. However, it is rarely so cut and dry. Rather than having a very clear and logical organizational structure with the project manager at the top, there may be multiple managers overseeing different regional or functional teams and it may be only very loosely defined on how these teams interact and are accountable to each other.

As we learned in the section on Support Activities, every LSP is different in how they choose to set up their internal structure. This book is not meant to dictate the best possible way to do this. However, an LSP should always be structured so as to empower the project manager to deliver value to the clients.

Every day project managers have to deal with other internal teams in order to accomplish their project goals. This could be negotiating with the finance department on acceptable margins in order to get a new project approved or dealing with an engineering team offshore to get more support for a project. The challenge here is that the project manager does not have direct control over these teams. In a direct reporting structure, a project manager can simply give orders and completely control the entire process, but in a situation where there are other internal groups involved, it is not so simple. It requires a certain degree of diplomacy to get things done.

The downside to having decentralized internal teams is certainly less control over the end-to-end process, but the advantages can be significant. If a project manager does not have to manage the resources directly, his time is freed up to focus on managing resources rather than people. For example, if a project needs 23 hours of engineering work done, then he can request 23 hours of engineering work. She doesn't need to worry about who is providing the work—just whether or not the work will get

done. She doesn't have to care so much if the engineer is happy about the work, if they are having a bad day, or need to take some time off because their dog is sick. She doesn't have to worry about what that engineer is going to do for the remaining 17 hours in the week. All the project manager needs to worry about is the work request. This allows him to essentially remove the headache of having to deal with the people, so that he can focus on managing the resources that the people provide.

Don't get us wrong here: we do not suggest that people should be treated like just another resource. People are absolutely a company's number one asset and need to be treated well by an organization, especially in the language services industry. In the example above, we would assume that the poor engineer with the sick dog is being managed by a local team lead or engineering manager who has the time to properly motivate and manage that employee. It is crucial that this people management function still exists and this is why we have the Support Activities. In an organization that has decentralized internal team members, it simply means that the people management function is taken out of the hands of the project manager so that she can focus on managing the project and not people.

External Team Members (Supply Chain)

In the previous sections, we discussed the advantages and disadvantages of project managers working with direct reports and with other internal teams. In addition to managing internal team members, it is also the project manager's responsibility to manage external team members.

Typically in an LSP, the actual language services are outsourced to either smaller SLSPs or CLPs, as we discussed in the section on

Structure of the Industry. Managing external resources can present some unique challenges and benefits that the project manager needs to be aware of.

The major benefit of managing external resources, whether they are SLSPs or CLPs, is that you are their client. In such a relationship, you would seem to have a higher degree of control over what gets done and when, since you are the one holding the purchase order. Just like with direct reports, the external vendor works for and is accountable to the project manager. The only difference is that with direct reports, the project manager is the boss, whereas with external  resources, the project manager is the client. This means that in many regards, the project manager sets the terms of relationship and, just as with decentralized internal teams, does not need to worry about people management and can focus strictly on managing resources. The project manager sets the deadlines and clearly outlines the expectations to the external team members. So this means the project manager pretty much has all the control in such a relationship, right?

Wrong. The difference between managing direct reports and internal team members and external vendors is that vendors can (and frequently do) say no. So while the project manager would seem to hold a lot of power in such a relationship, they only hold as much power as the external team members are willing to give them. This is one of the biggest challenges of managing external resources. Again, a certain degree of diplomacy is involved here and a project manager often finds himself in the position of having to negotiate with vendors for every project, all the while trying to keep them happy. If the project manager treats the external team members poorly, he will soon find himself in a position where he cannot deliver on the projects because all his vendors are refusing to work with him.

An argument could be made that much of the responsibility for managing these vendor relationships should fall on the vendor manager, which is somewhat true. A smart project manager will work closely with the vendor manager to make sure the supply chain is functional and productive. But at the end of the day, it is the responsibility of the project manager to deliver the projects, and therefore it is the responsibility of the project manager to also make sure the supply chain is healthy and able to do this.

Time

After managing people, the second resource that a project manager is responsible for is time. Every project comes with a deadline and it is the job of the project manager (or whoever is carrying out the project management Core Function) to make sure that deadline is met.

Most activities in our industry take a set amount of time, with very little variation. There are standard throughput metrics that are generally accepted throughout the industry. Desktop publishing specialists can format 10 pages per hour. Translators can translate 2,000 words per day. An experienced translator will undoubtedly be able to translate more words per day than an inexperienced translator, but the difference in throughput is not going to be that big. Similarly, engineering tasks, testing, quality assurance, and other necessary project tasks are going to have pretty standardized throughputs throughout the industry. So if most tasks in the industry are standard, then shouldn't all LSP's be pretty equal in their ability to deliver projects on time?

Companies are able to differentiate themselves on timelines through effective project management. Sure, throughputs for translated words per hour may be pretty consistent across the industry, but how those translation projects are managed is where companies are able to really set themselves apart. Think about it: a translator can translate 2,000 words per day, but a typical 2,000-word project can take anywhere from a couple of hours to a couple of weeks. This is because there are a lot of other moving pieces to the project that need to be scheduled and managed by the project manager.

Figure 21: The impact of proper and poor planning on the timeline of a translation project.

Looking at the lifecycle of a typical translation project, the majority of the time is spent with a file waiting in somebody's inbox waiting for work to begin. A client emails a file for translation to an LSP, where it sits for a couple hours until project manager opens the file. She then emails it to an engineer, with whom it sits for a few more hours. The file eventually whizzes off to a translator, who ignores it for a few more hours before declining the project, so the file is sent to another translator. And so on… All of this and not a single word has been translated yet.

The challenge here is not the speed at which tasks can be performed, but rather the efficiency with which multiple tasks can be managed. The project manager is responsible for setting the schedule and planning and allocating resources in the correct amounts and at the correct times to ensure that the project keeps moving forward. The better the project management, the less time that file will spend sitting in somebody's inbox, and the sooner it will be delivered to the customer.

Technology

One of the ways a project manager can ensure the project moves forward in the most efficient way possible is by making sure the right technology is used throughout the project. There are so many different types of technology available, it is impossible to list them all here. We could even include things as simple as calendars, Gantt charts, and tracking spreadsheets. But there are three major classes of technology that the project manager should always have at their disposal when managing a localization project: project management technology, computer-aided translation (CAT) tools, and machine translation.

Project Management Technology

Project managers must rely upon some sort of technology to help them keep track of their projects. This is especially true in the language services industry because the majority of localization projects have the added complexity of being managed for multiple markets at once. A software development project manager has one product to manage, but when that product is sent for localization into 10 languages, the LSP project manager now has 10 projects to manage. This can quickly become overwhelming if the project manager is not using some sort of technology to help track the progress of each project. Emails will keep piling up and the project manager can't keep up.

Some LSPs develop their own in-house project management software, which tracks project status from start to finish. Other LSPs choose to purchase third party software. As CAT tools evolved over time, many of the leading tools that are already used for translation now have built-in components to help manage workflow and provide real-time reporting.

However, if LSPs do not have the money to invest in fancy project management software, there are options. You may not need to buy the yacht just to cross the lake. There are a number of open source (free) products available that offer basic project management functionalities. We would encourage each project manager to search and see what is out there.

Or if simplicity is the goal, there is absolutely nothing wrong with simply tracking projects in a spreadsheet. This is such a common practice, you may not even consider it "technology", but it most certainly is! The project manager's job is to manage the project in the most efficient way possible and she has a responsibility to utilize any technology to that end, whether that is an expensive project management software suite or just a humble spreadsheet.

Oversimplified Project Tracking Spreadsheet

Project Name	Received	Sent to Translator	Received from Translator	Sent to Proofreader	Received from Proofreader	Final Quality Check	Delivered to Client
Sample Project #1	13 Apr	13 Apr	14 Apr	14 Apr	15 Apr	15 Apr	15 Apr
Sample Project #2	14 Apr	14 Apr	16 Apr	17 Apr	18 Apr		
Sample Project #3	15 Apr	15 Apr	15 Apr	15 Apr	16 Apr	16 Apr	16 Apr
Sample Project #4	15 Apr	16 Apr	18 Apr	18 Apr			

CAT Tools and Machine Translation

CAT tools are by far the most crucial piece of technology available in the industry. These are powerful tools in the hands of an experienced project manager. For the uninitiated, we will explain: CAT tools are able to take content from virtually any type of file and put them into a translation-friendly environment for translators to work on. In addition, they automatically create and maintain translation memories (TMs), which are large databases of previously translated content. Thus, you can leverage content translated in the past and not have to translate everything from scratch for each new project. Really, a whole book can be written on this technology, but that is not what we are trying to do here. Our focus here is on how CAT tools can be a powerful asset for project managers.

CAT tools and their various features are usually managed by more experienced localization engineers who specialize in this technology. But an experienced project manager should have at least a basic working knowledge of the different CAT tools on the market and the strengths and weaknesses of each one. Ultimately, she will be responsible for defining the strategy around which CAT tools to use in which circumstances. This decision will impact the amount of time spent by the localization engineers managing the CAT tools and the file processing, and it will also impact how efficiently the translators are able to work. Furthermore, by taking advantage of the TMs, the project manager is able to have more control over costs, as the TMs can greatly decrease the amount of words that need to be translated.

There are also a number of tools available that allow for automated quality assurance checks to be performed on translated content. Sometimes, this functionality is built into the CAT tools. So, this should be taken into account when selecting which CAT tool to use. Other times, though, these automated checks are either third party applications or developed internally in LSPs. Regardless of the source, it is the project manager's responsibility to ensure that such tools are being utilized in order to ensure high quality deliverables to the client.

In addition to CAT tools, there is also the availability of machine translation (MT), which is becoming more and more ubiquitous in the industry. There are a lot of misconceptions out there surrounding what MT is and what it isn't. We have pointed out that it is not a magic wand. MT is not a replacement for translation. Instead, it is a tool that can be used only under certain circumstances to increase translation throughput and lower costs.

An experienced project manager will have a working knowledge of how MT can be implemented in their projects in order to add value to the customer.

Money

We like making money. That's why we took some of your money in exchange for this book. We are going to go out on a limb here and speculate that most people are like us in this regard. The language services industry certainly has a lot of people who are truly passionate about what they do and this has inspired many people to go out and start their own companies. However, passion does not pay the bills and at the end of the day a company (or an individual) needs to make a profit for their activities or they will go out of business.

Margin is king. If you are not making a margin on the work that you are doing, you are working for free. Many companies fail because they are not able to make a margin on the services they provide and usually this is because nobody understands whose responsibility it is to look after this margin. Is this the responsibility of the sales team to negotiate higher selling rates with the clients?

Is it the responsibility of the finance team to manage assets and overhead cost allocation better? Is it the responsibility of the supply chain manager to negotiate lower costs with suppliers? Please allow us to clarify here: project margin is the sole responsibility of the project manager.

Before you get your torches and pitchforks out, let us just say: As we are writing this, we are cringing. Well, Tucker is cringing. Renato is cheering. This is because Tucker comes from a project management background and this is forcing him to think back on all the unprofitable projects he has managed throughout his career and take personal responsibility for that. Renato comes from a sales background and is tired of hearing project managers complain about the sales team not negotiating higher rates. So allow us to clarify what we mean here, so that we can put some of our project managers readers at ease.

When we say that margin is the project manager's responsibility, we mean that once a contract is signed and work commences, the project manager (or whoever is carrying out the project management Core Function) is the one person who is in the position to either make or lose money on that project. That is because the project manager manages all the resources for the project, as we have been discussing above. Mismanagement of people, time, or technology means that costs will exceed revenue and the company will lose money.

Sure, sometimes the project manager is set up to fail because of factors outside of his control. In such a case, it is usually because there is a lack of support from one or more of the seven LSP Support Activities (management, structure, culture, finance, facilities, HR, and quality assurance). Sometimes it is the failure on the part of the other Core Functions, such as when the sales team closes a deal and agrees to rates that are too low, or the vendor manager is not effectively negotiating with the vendors. These are all reasons why a project may lose money, but they are not excuses. At the end of the day, like it or not, margins are the responsibility of the project manager. We are not necessarily saying that this is always fair. We understand this.

The project manager is the one who creates a project budget to maximize revenue and reduce costs. To maximize revenue, she will be the one to provide quotes to the client and negotiate rates. To reduce costs, she must assign resources and  make sure they stay on track and take advantage of available tools and technology to streamline processes and reduce costs. All this rests on the shoulders of the project manager.

The Sales Core Function

The third Core Function of the language services provider is sales. Just as with our discussions about project management and vendor management, it is important to clarify here that we are discussing a function, not a role. The Core Functions of vendor management and project management can be performed by different people, but they are traditionally carried out either by dedicated vendor managers or project managers. The sales Core Function is by far the furthest reaching function in that it is carried out by the widest variety of people in an LSP. Sales is a function that happens (or should happen) every single time a customer or potential customer interacts with, hears about, or talks about your company.

Sales happens whenever a project manager delivers a file, somebody reads an email from your marketing team, or hears a speech at a conference from your CEO. Everybody in the company is responsible for sales. If a junior engineer does great work, the client is happy and will consider doing more business with the company. That is sales. If a vendor manager is able to quickly staff a new project through a complex strategic vendor management strategy, the client may go to a conference and tell colleagues at other companies about the great recruiting abilities of your company. That is sales. And of course, when an actual salesperson reaches out to prospective new clients to better understand what international challenges they are currently facing, that is sales, too.

For the sake of simplicity, though, in this section we will be referring to the salesperson as the one responsible for carrying out many of these activities. As with project management, where there are many different people within the company who work together to manage a project but the activities are coordinated by the project manager, it's the same in sales. While sales is carried out by many different people within an LSP, it is often ultimately the salesperson's responsibility to coordinate such activity in such a way that it leads to increased revenue for the company.

There are many ways to approach sales. Airport bookstores around the globe are lousy with paperbacks touting advice and strategies on how to win more customers and grow your business. This is not one of those books. This is not a book about how to increase Sales activity because that is not the book that we wanted to write. We wanted to write a book about how to navigate the language services industry. Therefore, we will be skipping over a lot of Sales Theory so that we can focus better on the concepts that are either unique to or especially important in the language services industry.

That having been said, it is important to note that for any LSP, an effective sales strategy is crucial to its long-term success as a profitable company. We have already discussed in our Market Influencer evaluation that the language services industry is a very small industry with a high degree of emphasis on brand equity. Your salespersons are your primary brand equity ambassadors. They have the power to greatly influence your reputation within the industry for better or for worse.

There is much to gain by having a successful sales strategy. This is why it is categorized along with vendor management and project management as one of the three Core Functions of the LSP. However good the vendor management and project management teams are, it won't matter if there are no customers for them to service. The sales team is the one responsible for bringing in those new clients and growing revenue for the company.

A competent, experienced, and well-connected salesperson is worth their weight in gold in the language services industry. An experienced salesperson will not only come with industry knowledge, but also a rolodex full of connections to start working on day one. This is not an area where you want to try to save some money by hiring inexperienced or unqualified salespersons. Hire the best and pay them well, for they are going to hold the keys to landing new clients and growing the business. We mentioned above that sales is a function and not a role, and therefore it can, in theory, be carried out by any team member in the organization. However, when it comes to new business, we would highly recommend that as soon as your company is making enough money to support it, you hire a full-time experienced sales team. You will not be sorry.

We have seen LSPs struggle with growth because they either do not or cannot maintain a good sales team. Usually this is for one of two reasons. Either they do not want to pay the big bucks for top performing salespersons, or the senior management doesn't fully respect the complexity and value of sales, thinking they can do it themselves. Technically, they are not wrong. The CEO of an LSP is, of course, free to hire junior salespersons or simply do all the selling himself. Either way, though, the end result is an inexperienced and ineffective sales team. LSPs can survive a long time with an inexperienced sales team, but will continually struggle to grow in a meaningful way until they make the decision to invest fully in this area.

Adding Value through the Sales Core Function

You may be wondering why we classify sales as a Core Function rather than a Support Activity. In any other industry, we would have the same feeling as sales usually exists only to win new business. Yes, they increase revenue, but they don't particularly add value for the end customer. Once they have closed a deal, they turn everything over to the production teams and go on to find their next deal.

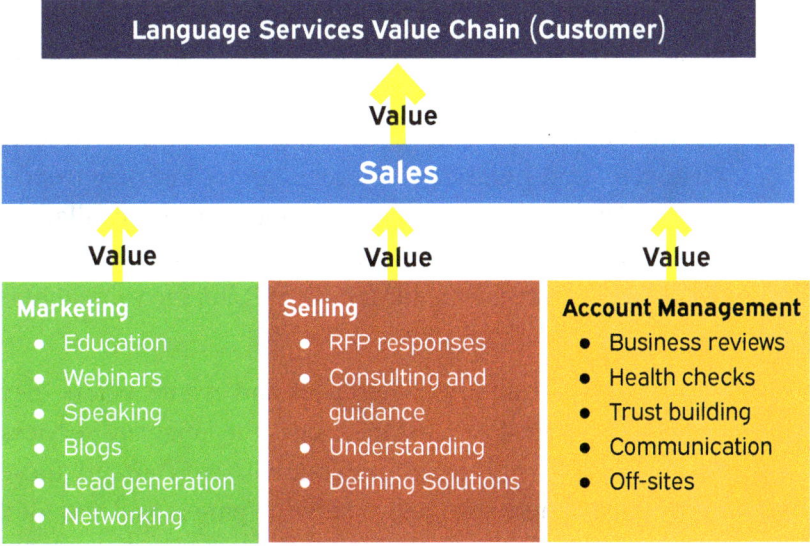

Figure 22: The Sales Core Function adds value to the customer through marketing, selling, and account management.

In the language services industry, however, sales cannot operate like this. When a deal is closed, there is still a continued need for sales. Why? Because the industry is incredibly complex and therefore not well understood by many end customers. Remember, LSBs, by definition, are not part of the industry. They come to LSPs when they need to purchase language services. Therefore, most LSBs are approaching the industry as total outsiders and they need somebody to guide them through this process.

Sales adds value through marketing, selling, and account management. Marketing begins before the client is even ready to buy language services. Once they are interested in purchasing language services, the selling activities begin. Once that customer is onboarded and rolling, the sales Core Function takes place through account management activities. As you can see, the sales Core Function never ends. It starts before the customer even signs a contract and continues (hopefully) indefinitely.

Marketing

The overall sales process starts with marketing, which provides information to LSBs and potential LSBs not just about a particular LSP, but about the industry as a whole. Take a look at any mature LSP's website and you will see a vast library of learning materials aimed towards their customers. LSPs host webinars to educate their customers and potential customers about industry trends. They write blogs suggesting ways to approach key challenges faced by LSBs. Of course, this is marketing material, so the primary objective is to generate new leads for the LSP, but the value that is added is the education they provide.

LSPs also attend industry conferences and events, where they meet other LSPs as well as LSBs to discuss the language services industry. Sales and marketing professionals who attend these events are often keynote speakers or serve on panels well attended by people hungry for more information. They meet with potential clients to understand their needs and suggest possible courses of action to those who need guidance. Thus, the sales team has added value even before the customer ever sends a request for proposal (RFP), and regardless of whether or not they actually ever do business together.

Selling

The selling role is what most people think of when they think of salespersons. The image of the seedy used car salesman comes to mind. Or perhaps people can't get Glengarry Glen Ross out of their minds. If you're too young to get the reference, Google it. You won't be sorry.

The reality is that sales is so much more than just closing the deal. Sales is working with a potential customer to understand their needs and then guide them through the complex world of the language services industry, for it can be intimidating to an outsider. Salespersons need to play the part of teacher, referee, coach, and motivational speaker. Being expert communicators, they are able to have a conversation with the client to understand what their core needs are, take these requirements to their production teams (usually the project manager) to find a solution, and then communicate this back to the client. Through this process, the customer is able to understand not only what the LSP is proposing, but also their own challenges in a completely new light.

Account Management

Once a potential customer becomes an actual customer, the sales Core Function takes the form of account management. Some LSPs assign this function to the project management team, while other LSPs have official account managers who are responsible for one or more clients. Of course, a key responsibility of these account managers is to develop and grow the business. In this regard, they operate largely under the same principles as the sales team that did the original selling.

An additional responsibility of account managers is managing the customer relationship. They maintain good communication with the customers through regular check-ins, quarterly business reviews (QBRs), and regular meetings. Building trust allows the LSP to make sure their clients remain happy and also provides a better understanding of the customers' needs. By understanding the customers better, LSPs are able to continuously identify new areas where they can add even more value.

Now that we understand how the sales Core Function adds value through marketing, selling, and account management, we would like to have a deeper discussion around how LSPs approach sales. It is not our intention to write a comprehensive guide on how to do sales, though. In the following sections we outline some key concepts that LSPs need to keep in mind to successfully add value (and grow their business).

Ways to Increase Business

It is ultimately the job of the sales Core Function to grow revenue for the business. This is such an important function that the salesperson typically works on commission, meaning that the amount of money he makes is directly tied to how much new revenue he is able to grow for the company. There are countless books written on the subject and many of them will  outline new and innovative strategies for exactly how to go about growing business. For the purposes of this book, though, we prefer to keep it simple.

There are, at the most basic level, only three ways of growing business. You can increase the number of clients you have, increase the average size of sale per client, or increase the number of times a client returns to buy again. That's it. As with most simple concepts, the devil is in the details. What makes this more complicated is that, in a typical LSP, these three ways of growing business are often pursued by entirely different team members. Marketing professionals focus on marketing and lead generation, salespersons manage the selling process, and account management can be carried out by project managers, account managers, salespersons, or a combination of any of these.

Growing Revenue by...	Responsible Parties
New Clients	Sales Team, Marketing, Solutions Architects
Upselling	Account Managers, Project Managers, Solutions Architects, Technology Teams
Customer Retention	Project Managers, Engineers, Vendor Management, Technology Teams

A coordinated sales strategy considers each of these three ways of growing business and makes sure that all responsible parties act in synch with each other to accomplish the common goal of increasing revenue for the company. Let's explore each of these functions in a little bit more detail below.

Increasing the Number of Clients

When most people think of sales, they think of talking to prospective clients and convincing them to purchase your services. That is to say they think of the selling process. This is perhaps the easiest and simplest way to quickly grow a business, but it will require investment into dedicated salespersons who are tasked with the responsibility of landing new clients.

Though the salesperson is the CEO of his sales pipeline, the selling process frequently involves other departments as well. It is especially critical that salespersons be well supported to provide the expert consulting and education to add value to potential customers. Selling is a consultative role and potential customers are looking for expertise. It is impossible for any single salesperson to know everything, so they need to be fully supported by project managers, engineers, solutions architects, and other team members. Selling in the language services industry is a team effort.

SELLING IS A TEAM EFFORT IN THE LANGUAGE SERVICES INDUSTRY.

What this means, in practical terms, is that there is no room for friction between the sales and production teams. They need to work together seamlessly. The LSPs that are able to close quality deals and have long-term relationships with their customers are the ones that have the best teamwork between sales and production. As we have said, the Sales Core Function is the decentralized of the Three Core Functions and it requires all responsible parties to be working together in harmony.

When talking to a potential new customer, a seasoned salesperson does not wait long to invite members of the production team to the conversation. He knows that he will need to rely on their experience and input if they must address the customer's questions and concerns. Adding value through the selling process is a true team effort in the language services industry, and it is the salesperson's job, as the CEO of his pipeline, to assemble and lead the team towards the common goal of closing new business.

Increasing the Average Size of Sale per Client

The simplest way of increasing the average size of sale per client is to raise prices, so that existing customers pay more for each project. If we do that, though, there is the risk that those clients may leave and go find a cheaper vendor. So we could also try to sell additional services to our existing customers. This is a sales strategy that is so pervasive in our everyday life, most of us don't even think of it as sales. If you've ever eaten fast food, you've surely been on the receiving end of the question, "So you have ordered the number four, would you like fries with that?" It is as simple as that, except it is more like, "So you have ordered the translations, would you like in-country search engine optimization consulting with that?"

As an example, let's look at a small SLSP in Montreal that provides French Canadian translations. While not as greedy as their American neighbors, they are still capitalists and would like to make more money so they can buy more flannel hats or hockey pucks or whatever it is Canadians spend their money on. So, given that their customers are already buying French Canadian translations from them, the LSP could try and see if they would also be interested in paying for testing or copywriting services. It is difficult to tell what their existing clients may want to buy from them, and surely many of the clients will not be interested in buying additional services at all. However, they will never find out if the sales Core Function is not carried out.

Another way to upsell is to ask the clients if they would like to upgrade existing services to premium level. Rather than, "Would you like fries with that?" you are asked, "Would you like to supersize that?" And, this is where the LSP asks if its customers would be interested in adding an additional round of review by specialized copy editors. For an additional 20%, of course.

In this example, it may not be the salesperson's job to get involved at all. Perhaps it is better that project managers have a discussion with customers to understand where there may be additional opportunities. Since the project managers are already engaging with customers, presumably they have already built a certain degree of trust in their relationships. So, they are better suited to have this conversation than a salesperson the client has perhaps never even met before.

Because this is a job that is not usually in the hands of the salesperson, sadly it often gets overlooked. Salespersons are hungry, always looking for new business. Sometimes they are literally hungry, if they are working on commission and therefore depending on their sales to put bread on the table. Project managers are focused on providing good service and are not always looking to add more to their already long list of responsibilities. Furthermore, remember that project managers are responsible for margin. This means that they may be reluctant to add risky new services that may cause their margin to drop.

It is, therefore, important to make sure that all client-facing team members within an LSP have a basic level of sales training. If not, you are surely leaving money on the table. The potential payoff for providing this training vastly outweighs the costs. Think about how many times you've paid for fries that you didn't even want. Now think about how little effort it took for that teenager to sell them to you. He just needed to be properly trained to ask the question.

Customer Retention

Another way to increase your revenue is to increase the number of times your customers return to buy from you, or what is called customer retention or loyalty. Most LSPs do not even think of this as part of sales, because it is pretty much a given that customers will return to purchase more services so long as they are kept happy. Because of this, there is usually very little involvement from the sales team in this process. It is typically a task given to account managers who add value by managing the customer relationship, making sure their needs are met, and that they are happy customers who will keep coming back. But just because this is typically performed by account managers and not salespersons, it doesn't mean that it is any less a part of the sales Core Function.

We already looked at customer retention during our Market Influencer evaluation when we discussed the ease (or cost) of switching providers. As we stated back then, ensuring that your customers will stay with you for the longer term is a function of the total value you bring to the customer and the perceived cost of switching vendors (stickiness). Value is created through your core competencies by providing excellent service to the customer. Perceived switching cost is increased as you become more and more embedded into the customer's process, whether that be through process knowledge, technology, or relationships.

Although customer retention is an important part of the sales Core Function, it is not carried out by the sales team. This is because customers don't return to buy more because of the salesperson, but because of the value they get from project management and vendor management Core Functions. Full responsibility for customer retention lies on the shoulders of the production team.

Increasing Value	Increasing Stickiness
Good communication	Integrated technology
On-time delivery	Specialized/trained resources
High quality	In-house process knowledge
Good value/cost ratio	Proprietary technology

Attacking on Multiple Fronts

We outlined the three basic ways that an LSP can grow business. This may seem like common sense, but we assure you that in this case at least, common sense isn't so common. Even when LSPs have a sales strategy, they do not think strategically about customer retention and upselling as a way to increase their company's growth. Rather, they focus their efforts on new client acquisition, and in many cases, do quite a poor job of it because senior management either doesn't respect the sales Core Function or they are trying to cut corners by hiring inexpensive Salespersons. It is for this reason that we wanted to highlight each of these areas and outline the importance of having a strategy for each of them.

Most LSPs believe that if they are going to grow by 30%, they need to win 30% more customers. So if your baseline is 100 clients who do two transactions per year at an average of $10,000 per transaction, your total revenue would look like this:

100 clients x $10,000 per transaction x 2 transactions/year = $2 million in total revenue

If you were to increase the number of clients by 30%, your revenue would increase 30% accordingly, of course.

130 clients x $10k per transaction x 2 transactions/year = $2.6 m in total revenue (30 %)

This is certainly one way to accomplish the goal, but not necessarily the easiest or the smartest. Rather than giving your sales team the challenging task of 30% year-over-year growth, this responsibility can be spread out to various teams within the organization. Instead of aiming to increase the number of clients by 30%, you could increase the number of clients by 10%, increase the number of transactions per client by 10%, and increase the size of each sale by 10%. For example, next year your sales team wins 10% more clients, your account management team convinces your existing clients to buy 10% more services, and your project management team provides excellent service so the clients return to buy 10% more in ongoing services. This would look something like this:

110 clients x $11k per transaction x 2.2 transactions/year = $2.662 m in total revenue (~33 % increase)

As you can see, by spreading out the effort and responsibility for the sales function across the organization and focusing not just on new business, we are actually able to see a projected increase of over 33% in revenue. This requires only a third of the selling effort and a 10% increase in the productivity of each function.

Think Big

Renato has worked for LSPs large and small. He has started his own translation companies, grown them, and sold them off so he could move on to the next challenge. He has been plugged into language services for decades and has watched the rise of Massive Multiple Language Services Providers within the industry. Tucker, likewise, has worked for small startups, medium-sized companies, and large companies. Both of us have certainly seen LSPs struggle with growth and we have seen promising companies fail because they are not able to scale sustainably. This is because LSPs think small. Rather than embracing the global nature of the industry, LSPs all too often choose to place artificial limits on themselves by thinking of themselves as just another small company in a global industry.

We've seen salespersons struggle and get frustrated because they are trying to grow the business but are fighting against the internal culture of their company. Sometimes an LSP grows their business but fails to grow their thinking, which is old-fashioned or perhaps overly conservative. Because of this, the responsibility to drive aggressive growth and visionary thinking often falls on the sales team.

If you are reading this as a senior manager or owner of an LSP, please pay attention. It is the role of the management to set culture and to support the Core Functions. By creating a visionary and forward-thinking culture, you will be setting up your teams to add much more value. If you are reading this as a salesperson, then buckle up, because you've got work to do.

Historically, LSPs tend to be started by entrepreneurs that either came from linguistic or project management backgrounds. It is essential for founders and CEOs to grow out of the mindset of a linguist or project manager and start thinking more strategically. One of the tools we have discussed is setting the company's vision through writing a vision statement for the company. A small LSP without a vision statement will all too often fall into a mindset that limits their potential. For example, below is something that we hear in the industry all too often when speaking with LSP sales teams.

"We are a Small Ukrainian Translation Agency."

In 2013, Renato gave a talk at the first-ever Ukrainian localization conference, titled "We are a Small Ukrainian Translation Agency." The talk was about how LSPs can be their own worst enemies by failing to embrace their global potential in the global language services industry. This is why the Support Activities of management and culture need to be aligned so as to support the sales Core Function to add value and grow the company.

We talk about it here in the context of the sales Core Function because it is the sales team that is driving aggressive growth for an LSP. However, this discussion may be interesting to anybody in the language services industry, particularly CEOs or LSP owners looking to expand their business globally.

Of course, you can replace the word Ukrainian with Polish, French, American, or Korean. Just as how you can substitute the word "translation" with "interpretation", "staffing" or "multimedia". The location and the type of work of the company doesn't matter so much, but the sentence structure and spirit remains the same. Let's look at how the following words in this statement limit your mindset and prevent you from aggressively closing new business and expanding into new markets.

First, let's look at the word "small". This word is worse than meaningless when describing an LSP. By describing your LSP as

The General Theory of the Translation Company

small, all you are doing is limiting yourself by creating a perception for your buyers and employees that you cannot scale to meet global demand. Size doesn't matter for LSPs. Size is information that is totally irrelevant. Think about it. Do you go to a bank because it is a small bank or a big bank? Do you go to a restaurant because it is a small restaurant or a big restaurant? What information does that add to the conversation, especially for an industry like ours with such low barriers to entry and growth? Furthermore, size is completely subjective. A new LSP with 10 employees may feel small when they compare themselves to a larger company with 100 employees, but that larger company with 100 employees certainly feels the same way when they look at a company with 1,000 employees.

Thinking small is indicative of a two-fold inferiority complex that is pervasive in the language services industry. Firstly, we industry insiders tend to misguidedly think that our industry is small and unimportant. Secondly, we think of our individual companies as small within the context of the larger industry. This is utter nonsense. Forget the word small. Never say it. LSPs, by nature, are global companies that have the ability to scale very quickly compared to other industries. Small LSPs only win business from small customers, so you should never brand yourself as a small company. Size does not matter in this industry. You are not small, you are global.

Secondly, we are going to look at the word "Ukrainian", which describes the location of the headquarters. LSPs, as we said, are global companies. The location of their headquarters does not matter. Highlighting it only serves to limit your potential. Consider, for example, a Brazilian SLSP that provides Brazilian Portuguese translation services to MLSPs. They do pretty good business perhaps, but by branding themselves as a Brazilian translation agency, they have effectively destroyed the sales team's ability to win new revenue by selling additional languages to new and existing clients. For instance, many of their customers could have been convinced to purchase Spanish translations from them as well. For the customers, it would be one less vendor to deal with.

Remember that LSPs are global in nature and that if you limit yourself to a specific country or language, you are limiting your ability to add value through the sales Core Function.

The last word we are going to look at is the word "agency". This word is frightfully pervasive in the language services industry and is used by LSBs and LSPs alike. The reason that we take umbrage with this word is because it is not accurately representing the value that an LSP brings to their customers. Agencies are middlemen. The word agency simply means an intermediary. For example, let's look at a real estate agency. What value do they bring to the product? They serve as intermediaries between the seller and the buyer. At the end of the day, you are still buying the same house. There is very little value being added in this process.

For an LSP to brand themselves as an agency, they are effectively saying that they do not add any value to the process, which would be an absolute misrepresentation of the business. An LSP does so much more than just transfer files. Project managers create style guides and glossaries to ensure quality; vendor managers create value through strategic vendor management. This is why LSPs are not agencies, but service providers. Which is why we have been referring to them for over a 100 pages as language services providers.

Keeping these points in mind, let's look at the above statement and see how this can be improved. LSPs should never label themselves as small or limited to a specific region: they are global. And LSP is not an agency, they are a valuable service provider. LSPs facilitate global communication between the top companies in the word. They add value to their customers by using their expertise in global markets to lead them in their journey towards world dominance.

Good salespersons already know that you should never let the details get in the way of an opportunity. If anything, good salespersons will have a reputation of being a little too cocky. We are not implying that a salesperson should go out and lie to new customers about the size or scope of their company. Certainly not. But you don't have to bend the truth to realize the power and potential of an LSP. This isn't snake oil that we are selling, it is the reality. In today's language service industry, there is no such thing as a small local translation agency. We are all global service providers, so it is important to remember this and not let the industry's inferiority complex limit your growth.

Talk about Value, Not Price

We have discussed over and over again the fact that the language services industry is not about translations, but about adding value. LSPs do not simply provide translations (like an "agency"), they provide value-added services to their customers through the Core Functions.

No matter what your role in the company, your job is to enhance the value of the company. If you speak this language no matter who you are or what you are doing, then you are going to have a long and successful career in the industry. This is true for everybody from the entry-level translator to the CEO, but is by far the most important to the salesperson. While the sales Core Function perhaps is not responsible for creating the same type of value as the project management Core Function or the vendor management Core Function, the salesperson has an even more challenging job. The salesperson's job is to communicate this value to potential customers in a way so that value is understood and appreciated, and then hopefully leverage this understanding and appreciation into more business and increased revenue for the LSP.

This is why it is absolutely essential for the salesperson to know exactly what it is they are selling and the value they bring to the table. Of course, this is true in any industry, but we would argue that it is even more critical when selling language services. Remember, this is an industry that is misunderstood at best and completely devalued at worst in the eyes of the customer. When a car salesman is talking to a customer, there is a baseline understanding: everybody is aware of the various features available in a car and how these create value. The wheels go round and the engine goes vroom. Everybody is clear. When selling language services, the customer frequently is tragically under-informed about the services they are buying and so it is up to the salesperson to guide them through the process.

This takes the form of consulting services and information sharing. This is why so many marketing departments write dozens of blogs and host webinars to provide training to potential clients on the services they offer. By educating the client, they can both make the client more comfortable with the services they will be purchasing and also display the value that the LSP brings to the partnership. Sales can add value by educating the customer about the solution they are offering.

More effective, perhaps than trying to guide the customer towards the solution, though, is talking to them about their problem. Solutions can be complicated and it is not really necessary that the customer understands exactly how the sausage is made. Once the client has a better understanding of their problem, they can be convinced to accept your offer to help them with it. This requires building trust with the client first. If the client is going to trust you to take care of their problem without understanding exactly how you plan to do this, they need to trust that you have the skills and experience to do this. For example, the doctor doesn't need to educate every patient on the exact process he will use during the amputation. The doctor only needs to convince the patient of two things, that the foot has to come off and that he is qualified to make this happen.

Another way to keep the conversation focused on your value is to avoid talking about price. This can be tricky because many clients want to know the price first before they will even continue a conversation. This is the sign of a very immature buyer. The salesperson's challenge is to shift the conversation away from price and focus on the value that the LSP brings to the table. This value is communicated by speaking directly to the customer's needs, which is a two-way conversation. By having a conversation about the client's struggles, the salesperson is in a position to define a unique value proposition. Only once all parties fully understand the challenges faced and the proposed value-add solutions, are you ready to discuss price.

Ask, Don't Tell

Another reason that good salespersons don't talk about price is because it is much like putting the cart before the horse. Price cannot be discussed until the service is defined. The service cannot be defined until the customer's challenges are understood. These challenges cannot be understood until there is a conversation between the LSP and the customer. This conversation needs to be a discovery session where the LSP learns everything they can about the customer's challenges so that they can best define how they are going to add value to the process. During this conversation, a wise salesperson will refrain from boasting about solutions.

You may think this is only necessary when selling to large and complex end-customers and so only applies to MLSPs dealing with top LSBs in the world. This is far from the truth. The truth is that this is a necessary conversation regardless of where you find yourself in the supply chain. An SLSP that is selling translation services to an MMLSP may think that it is not necessary to ask questions and understand the challenges and concerns of their customer. They may think that the MMLSP is only interested in price. This may be true, or it may not.

Mature vendor managers look for vendors based on their best value. As part of their evaluation, the client outlines what they are looking for in a vendor. For example, perhaps quality is prioritized higher than price, or timeliness is prioritized over experience. By asking questions to the MMLSP, the SLSP is able to understand how they will be evaluated as a vendor. This allows them to adapt their strategy accordingly in order to win more business from them.

By asking questions, you understand more about the maturity of your customer and how they view themselves. This is useful information for the salesperson, as it gives him more insight into how he should approach each customer. When we discuss buyer maturity, we are essentially talking about where the client sits on the spectrum between complete naivety to in-depth experience in buying language services. Naive, immature customers will be uninformed about how LSPs add value and will need to be guided through the process. Experienced, mature customers will know what they are about and so the conversation can be more strategic. It is important to understand the maturity of each customer in the language services industry, because, unlike other industries, you cannot take for granted that the customer is well-informed about what they are buying.

It is also useful to understand where the client thinks they land on the maturity spectrum. We have dealt with many clients who thought they knew what language services was all about, but were actually either under-informed or entirely misinformed. These can be difficult customers to sell to because they are not interested in discussing value or entertaining vendor suggestions on how to add more value. They think they know everything already and want to just buy based on price. Likewise, there are many clients who are all too happy to admit they are inexperienced when it comes to localization and so can humbly approach an LSP and ask for expert advice.

Customers are either mature or immature buyers of language services, but aren't always aware of their own maturity. Generally, clients fall into one of four categories, as outlined below.

	Immature	**Mature**
Thinks they are mature	**Downside:** Client is unteachable and may be resistant to introducing new improvements to their processes. **Upside:** Client is usually vested in localization, even if they are not using mature processes. You can channel this enthusiasm.	**Downside:** Not as much room for creativity. **Upside:** Consistency and efficiency. You can get right to business!
Doesn't think they are mature	**Downside:** It will take a long time to accomplish anything because you are essentially starting from scratch. **Upside:** All parties are teachable and eager to learn new things.	**Downside:** Constant struggle to keep up with changing expectations. **Upside:** Challenging and exciting initiatives and always opportunities to build new things.

Asking questions to discover more about the needs of the customer is the driving principle in different sales strategies. It is certainly not a novel idea that we came up with. The reason we discuss it here is because of the nature of the language services industry. As we have made clear, many clients are not at all sure what they need. They only know that they have some challenges and they have been tasked with solving them. This means that a customer or potential customer may sometimes think they want to buy one thing, but after you find out more about their challenges and pain points, you may discover that they actually need something else entirely. This is an area where sales can actively add value. By helping the customer identify problems and proposing solutions to those problems, the sales function adds value to the customer before the contract is even signed.

Getting to Work!

Well, we have made it this far. Hopefully, we haven't lost too many of you over the last couple hundred or so pages. We would have loved to write a shorter book, but don't see how that would be possible. Honestly, there is a wide range of additional topics that we originally wanted to cover, but they just didn't make the final cut. Even some of the concepts we were able to cover could easily be expanded into full books just by themselves.

When we first started, we told you that this book was meant to accomplish two goals: to have fun and to provide much needed information about the language services industry.

As for the first goal, we can proudly report mission accomplished! We have had a lot of fun writing this book and have learned a lot through the process. If you found the book to be a little dry and boring through certain sections (we warned you!), then please accept our sincere apologies. We can fully empathize. If you spent an hour reading a particular chapter, we spent 40 hours writing it.

But at the end of the day, we have thoroughly enjoyed being able to sit down and spend some time passing on our experience.

Our second goal was to provide information. Well, we have given it our best shot. We are certainly hoping that you will walk away with at least a few useful nuggets that you can start applying to your own adventure in the language services industry. Not all of the information presented in this book will be useful to everybody, but we hope that everybody will have found something that spoke to them.

Whether you are an industry veteran or a young entrepreneur just getting started, whether you work for an LSP or are purchasing services from one, your journey is unique to you. No one book will have all the answers. This is an industry built on relationships, so go out and meet new people. Start a conversation with them. Remain enthusiastically skeptical and ask meaningful questions. Take a look at your Market Influencer evaluation. Identify your niche and how you can add value to the language services industry. Structure yourself in such a way as to optimize the value of your Core Functions. Go win some new clients. Struggle. Learn new things along the way and refine your process.

Whoever you are and wherever you are, we are excited for you. As we said on the first page, welcome to the language services industry! Surely, our paths will cross at some point. Until then, don't forget to have fun!

Acknowledgements

Our Special Thanks

This book is the consolidation of decades of interactions and experiences with amazing people all over the world. It would be impossible to name all the influences and inspirations that have shaped our views of the industry.

Renato would start by acknowledging his brothers, Angelo, Helcio, and Ricardo, his accomplices, who have always been there for him. Liane Lazoski, Renato's first and longest partner in business and in life, who shared with Renato his earliest and most important challenges. Maria Gabriela Morales, Renato's Argentinean partner in the dream of building something consequential in South America. Don DePalma, a friend and a mentor, who taught Renato how to use analytical skills and helped him to shape his view of the industry. Renato's co-host in the Globally Speaking Radio podcast, Michael Stevens. And of course, his bosses who guided and challenged him to go forward, Tom Blondi, Jim Lewis, Jaap van der Meer, and Tomáš Kratochvíl, thank you!

Together, we have had the privilege to work with hundreds of talented people, colleagues, clients, employees, and leaders with whom we have shared experiences and learned a thing or two. We will certainly forget many, so my apologies upfront. Anne-Marie Colliander Lind, Fabiano Cid, Arturo Quintero, Kateřina Janků, Libor Šafář, Roberto Ganzerli, Françoise Bajon, Cecilia

Piaggio, William Cassemiro, Ricardo Souza, Adriana Machado, Bill Smith, Val Ivonica, Robert Sarver, Adam Asnes, Paul Danter, Mark Klco, Erik Vogt, Jon Haas, Vera Richards, Jorge Marinho, Cecilia Maldonado, Tomáš Brejcha, Salvatore Giammarresi, Eric Woelfel, Gianni Davico, Benjamin Sargent, Nataly Kelly, João Roque Dias, Marco Trombetti, Anna Tatistcheff, Tracey Feick, Pavel Soukeník, Iris Orriss, Lori Thicke, Denise Spacinsky, Ulrich Henes, Michael Anobile, Vijayalaxmi Hegde, Brian Kelly, Vladimir Reiff, Shane Gretten, Hans Fenstermacher, Martin Drápal, Gabriel Karandysovsky, Tahar Bouhafs, Joe DiDamo, Michael Burns, Jessica Rathke, Max Troyer, Jon Ritzdorf, Lee Densmer, Melissa C. Bottomley-Gillespie, Aki Ito, Konstantin Dranch, Lu Ding, Jason Mao, Qiliang Cui, George Zhao, Xudong Cao, Rutsuko Noda DeBels, German Gallo, Tereza Dyerová, Bára Rejzková, Anna Colominas, Zino Chao, Takao Tanaka, David Frodsham, Jochen Hummel, Cecilia Enbäck, Martin Spethman, Henri Broekmate, Paula Shannon, Daniel Goldschmidt, Marina Mikhayleva, Teresa Marshall, Jeff Guillem, Henry Liu, Tea Dietterich, Sophie C. Solomon, and Fredy Gottesmann.

Finally, our special thanks to Donna Parrish and Luigi Muzii for their feedback on the early drafts of this book.

Glossary

Let's Define Some Terms Used

Account management: Account management, along with marketing and selling is one of the three main activities of the sales Core Function. Account management focuses on maintaining the relationship with and growing business from existing customers.

Agency: An agency, in the context used in this book, refers to a company that acts as an intermediary but adds little or no additional value to the value chain.

AutoLQA: Automated language quality assurance refers to any software or tool that provides fully or partially automated quality checks. For example, spell-check is an AutoLQA tool.

Bargaining power of customers: One of the five Market Influencers, it refers to the amount of negotiation power held by the customer in the language services value chain. Factors affecting the bargaining power of customers are availability of information, switching costs, buyer concentration and size of industry, price sensitivity of buyer, competition, and availability of substitutes.

Bargaining power of suppliers: One of the five Market Influencers, it refers to the amount of negotiation power held by players downstream in the language services value chain. Factors affecting the bargaining power of suppliers are differentiation, impact of inputs on cost and differentiation, substitute inputs, supplier concentration, employee solidarity, and competition with suppliers.

Best value: The net value that is added to an individual engagement from different factors that are weighted according to the requirements of the engagement and considering the sum of the actual and potential costs.

Brand equity: The result of brand awareness and brand reputation.

Brand loyalty: When a customer prefers to continue to work with a certain vendor. The loyalty is to the vendor, not the individuals working at the vendor.

Brand recognition: How well-known a company is in the industry.

Brand reputation: How good (or bad) people perceive a company's brand to be.

Capital investment costs: The total costs incurred in starting a new company in the language services industry.

CAT: Computer-aided translation. Tools used by translators to increase productivity. CAT tools take advantage of translation memories (TMs) to reduce the total word count to be translated and include features that help maintain quality and consistency of translations.

CAT tool: See "CAT".

CLP: Contract language professional. CLPs are players within the language services industry who work for themselves, typically selling their services to LSPs. By far the most common type of CLP is the translator, but anybody working on a freelance or short-term contract basis can be considered a contractor. For example, testers, engineers, and consultants can all be considered CLPs.

Core competencies: See "Core Functions".

Core functions: Core Functions are the key activities of an LSP that directly add value to the language services value chain. They include vendor management, project management, and sales. Core functions are supported by Support Activities and influenced by the Market Influencers.

Culture: Culture is one of the seven Support Activities critical to the LSP. Culture comes from the top. It is set by the senior management and can either support or hinder a company's ability to add value through the Core Functions.

Desktop publishing: Formatting documents, images, and other media types. Translations are often performed in CAT tools, and so the translator does not work directly in the original file format. Desktop publishing is therefore an essential part of the localization process to ensure that formatting for each language is error-free and attractive to the end user.

Differentiation: The process carried out by a company to distinguish their services from those of their competitors and become more attractive to potential customers.

Direct reports: Team members who report directly to somebody. For example, a project manager with five direct reports means that he not only manages those five people for project work, but he also has the power to hire, fire, and implement performance improvement plans.

Distribution channels: See "Supply Chain".

DTP: See "Desktop publishing".

Ease of switching providers: The ease with which a buyer can change vendors. Related to "stickiness".

Economies of scale: Cost savings gained by increasing volume of services provided.

External teams: Teams from outside of the LSP, downstream in the supply chain.

Facilities - Support Activity: Facilities (grouped with HR) is bbresponsible for maintaining and operating global presence and infrastructure to provide the global manpower needed to add value through the Core Functions. Works closely with HR to ensure that local regulations are considered in each location.

Finance - Support Activity: It's responsible for managing financial assets and supporting scalable, healthy growth.

Freelancer: See "CLP".

Government influence: The level and type of influence local governments have on business. Governmental policies on business differ from country to country.

Herfindahl-Hirschman Index (HHI): A widely accepted way of measuring market concentration. HHI is used in the private sector and by government regulatory agencies. HHI calculates an industry's market concentration by squaring the market share of each company in the market and adding them together. The resulting score can range from almost zero (fragmented market) to 10,000 (monopoly).

Human resources (HR): Human resources (grouped with facilities) is one of the seven Support Activities. HR is responsible for providing the global manpower necessary to carry out the Core Functions.

IKEAzation: Refers to the process of replacing content with instructional pictures to reduce word count, and therefore localization costs. Popularized by IKEA, it is considered a substitute service for translation.

Improvised vendor management: Managing the vendor supply chain in a reactive manner without any planning.

Indirect reports: Team members who do not report directly to somebody. For example, a project manager may not have anybody officially reporting to him, but still needs to rely on team members to manage projects. The team members that he delegates work to are his indirect reports.

Industry rivalry: One of the five Market Influencers. It refers to the amount and nature of rivalry between competitors in the language services industry. Factors affecting industry rivalry are: innovation, marketing expenditure, competitive strategy, LSP concentration ratio, and transparency.

Integration: The process of integrating software and tools with those of the client, usually to improve efficiency by removing human steps. Integration can be expensive and difficult, but can lead to increased stickiness with the customer.

Intellectual property: Intangible assets owned by a company that provide a competitive advantage. Can be ideas, processes, software, proprietary tools, copyrights, etc.

IP: See "Intellectual Property".

Language services consumer (LSC): The ultimate user of language services. Sometimes, LSCs and LSBs are the same, but LSCs are typically the clients of the LSB.

Language services provider (LSP): The term for the most generical description of a company providing language services in the language services industry. The term LSP can apply to subcategories of companies, such as SLSPs, MLSPs, RMLSPs, and MMLSPs.

Language services value chain: The interconnected, branching chain of buyers and suppliers that work together to deliver all the language services to the end client. Each supplier in the language services value chain adds value through their Core Functions to increase the value incrementally at each stage until it is delivered to the end client (LSB).

Language technology provider (LTP): A company that specializes in developing technology and software to be used in the language services industry, such as machine translation, computer-aided translation, project management software, automated language quality assurance, etc.

Localization department: The division of an LSB that is tasked with localization of content. Typically, these departments have been an afterthought and are not well supported. However, this is changing in the industry as we are starting to see more experienced and mature localization departments within LSBs.

Localization engineer: Typically reports to project managers and is responsible for processing files using CAT tools, and performing lower level project management Core Functions.

LSC: See "Language services consumer".

LSP: See "Language services provider".

LTP: See "Language technology provider".

Machine translation (MT): Translation that is performed automatically by a computer without the aid of human translators. MT continues to become more prevalent in the industry, but is not able to provide the level of quality required by many customers. MT is a very useful tool for improving efficiency in very specific situations, often in conjunction with post-editing (MTPE).

Machine translation post-editing: The human process of post-editing machine translated content so that it meets acceptable quality levels.

Management - Support Activity: It is arguably the most important of all the Support Activities and is responsible for setting strategy and vision.

Market Influencer evaluation: An analysis of the five Market Influencers to identify risks and opportunities for an individual

LSP in the language services industry. The evaluation is a necessary step to make informed decisions about how to set up Support Activities to optimize the value-creating Core Functions.

Market influencers: Market Influencers are based on Michael Porter's article in the Harvard Business Review, "The Five Competitive Forces That Shape Strategy". They are threat of new entrants, threat of substitutes, bargaining power of customers, bargaining power of suppliers, and competitive rivalry.

Marketing: It is one of the key activities of the sales Core Function, along with selling and account management. Marketing is responsible for generating new leads and educating potential clients about language services.

Massive multiple language service provider (MMLSP): A very large MLSP. There is no official classification system for what constitutes a "massive" MLSP, but typically MMLSPs perform millions of dollars' worth of services and work with the top LSBs in the industry.

MLSP: See "Multiple language service provider".

MMLSP: See "Massive multiple language service provider".

MT: See "Machine translation".

MTPE: See "Machine translation post-editing".

Multiple language service provider (MLSP): A class of LSP that provides services for multiple languages. Typically, MLSPs work directly with LSBs.

Net value: Net value is calculated for a vendor based on how they rank across different requirements such as price, timeliness, and quality. The net value is multiplied by value multipliers for each category during the best value evaluation to rank vendors for each specific project.

Niche: The specialized area in which an LSP competes within the language services industry. Because of the diverse nature of the industry, there are many ways for LSPs to differentiate themselves and compete in their individual areas.

Outsourcing: Companies can outsource activities that are non-essential. The language services industry has a lot of outsourcing (see "language services value chain"). Core Functions are the only functions in an LSP that cannot be outsourced.

Professional Employer Organization (PEO): Can be used to hire local employees in different countries without having to set up local business entities or account for local labor laws.

Personal brand equity: An individual's brand equity in the language services industry. This can be related to, but is not absolutely tied to, the brand equity of the individual's company.

Personal customer loyalty: The tendency of a customer to follow an individual, rather than a company. For example, if a project manager leaves an LSP to go work for a different LSP, customers may follow that project manager and choose to work with the new LSP as well.

Price: The dollar amount paid by the customer to purchase services. Price is equal to the value added through Core Functions, plus markup, plus perceived value.

Project management: Project management, along with vendor management and Sales, is one of the three Core Functions through which LSPs directly add value to the language services value chain. Project management consists of managing the resources of people, time, technology, and money. It is a function, not a role, so it is carried out by multiple individuals within an LSP, not just the project manager.

QMS: See "Query Management System".

Quality Assurance - Support Activity: It is meant to provide consistency and to ensure that deliverables meet the customer's standards.

Query management system (QMS): A structured system for tracking and reporting verified answers to queries during the translation process.

RMLSP: See "Regional multiple language service provider".

RMLSP: A category of MLSP that provides language services for a specific region or subset of languages.

Sales: Sales, along with vendor management and project management is one of the three Core Functions through which LSPs directly add value to the language services value chain. Sales consists of marketing, selling, and account management and adds value through education, communication, and consulting. Sales is a function, not a role, so it may be carried out by multiple individuals within an LSP, not just the salesperson.

Salesperson: The person responsible for carrying out the selling activity as part of the sales Core Function. Salespersons can have different responsibilities and can be involved with marketing and account management as well.

SCMS: See "Supply chain management system".

Selling: Marketing is one of the key activities of the sales Core Function, along with Selling and Account Management. Marketing is responsible for generating new leads and educating potential clients about language services.

Management team: The senior managers responsible for the management Support Activity of setting strategy and vision and influencing culture within an LSP.

Single language service provider (SLSP): An LSP that specializes in providing services in one language. Typically, SLSPs provide services to MLSPs, but may also engage directly with LSBs.

SLSP: See "Single language services provider".

Specific value multiplier (SVM): The weighted importance for each category defined during the best value evaluation.

Stickiness: The degree to which a customer is committed to a vendor relationship. Stickiness can be caused by customer loyalty, high switching costs, high levels of integration, or a number of other factors.

Strategic improvised vendor management: Improvised vendor management with structure and processes put into place so that an LSP can be prepared for new requests in an organized manner.

Strategic vendor management: A combination of structured vendor management and improvisation that allows an LSP to be prepared and plan ahead, as well as remain flexible to respond to unexpected customer needs.

Structure - Support Activity: The structure of an LSP is what allows them to take advantage of economies of scale as they grow.

Structured vendor management: A form of vendor management that provides structure and planning. It adds value by allowing LSPs to perform best value evaluations, be prepared for new customers in the sales funnel, negotiate prices with the supply chain, and better respond to needs of customers.

Substitutes: Services that are not part of the language services industry but may threaten to replace traditional language services. Examples are machine translation, crowdsourcing, automation, artificial intelligence, and IKEAzation.

Supplier: See "Vendor".

Supply chain: Refers to a company's vendors downstream in the language services value chain.

Supply chain management systems: A structured database for managing vendors in the supply chain. Ideally tracks availability, reliability, and net value for each vendor.

Supply chain manager: See "vendor manager".

Support activities: Support Activities are defined in the context of the Market Influencer evaluation to minimize risk and maximize opportunity for an LSP and optimize the ability to add value through the three Core Functions. The seven LSP Support Activities are management, structure, culture, finance, facilities/HR, technology, and quality assurance.

Technology - Support Activity: Technology increases efficiency so that the Core Functions can add more value.

The Jell-O effect: When the language services industry is squeezed by layoffs, recession, etc., it just expands further, much like how Jell-O squeezes through fingers when squeezed.

The small town effect: The language services industry is like a small town, where everybody knows each other and nobody can keep a secret.

Threat of new entrants: One of the five Market Influencers. Also called a barrier to entry, it is the threat that new companies will directly compete for customers. It is affected by the following factors: intellectual property, governmental influence and policy, brand equity, customer loyalty, ease of switching providers, differentiation, economies of scale, profitability, and capital investment costs.

Threat of substitutes: One of the five Market Influencers. This is the threat that customers will substitute existing services for different services from outside the industry (see "Substitutes"). It is affected by the following factors: availability of substitutes, quality and nature of service, pricing of substitutes, switching costs, difficulty of substitutes, and buyer behavior.

TM: See "Translation memory".

TMS: See "Translation management system".

Translation management system (TMS): TMSs provide content and file management through the localization project lifecycle. Various TMSs have different functions and capabilities, such as built-in project management tools, AutoLQA tools, MT, and TMs.

Translation memory (TM): A database of previously translated content that can be used to automatically translate similar content in the future, thus reducing the time and effort required from the translator (and therefore cost).

User interface (UI): ("UI localization" and "Software socalization" are often used interchangeably).

Value: Value is the benefit provided through the language services value chain. Each supplier in the value chain adds value through Core Functions.

Vendor: A supplier of services in the language services value chain.

Vendor management (Core Function): Vendor management, along with project management and sales, is one of the three Core Functions through which LSPs directly add value to the language services value chain. Vendor management consists of adding value through structured and strategic vendor management. It is a function, not a role, so it may be carried out by multiple individuals within an LSP, not just the vendor manager.

Vendor manager: The primary person responsible for carrying out the vendor management Core Function.